MW00916217

ISTANBUL TRAVEL GUIDE

Unlock The Timeless Charms Of The Heart Of
Turkey With Savvy Tips For Cultural Exploration,
Detailed Itineraries And Map Guide

Gianna McMillon

Copyright Page

Disclaimer

The information provided in this travel guidebook is based on personal experiences, research, and third-party sources. While efforts have been made to provide accurate and up-to-date information, the publisher and author make no representations or warranties of any kind, express or implied, about the completeness, accuracy, reliability, suitability, or availability with respect to the information, products, services, or related graphics contained in this guidebook for any purpose.

The inclusion of any third-party websites or services does not necessarily imply a recommendation or endorse the views expressed within them.

TABLE OF CONTENTS

INTRODUCTION

Welcome to Istanbul, where the collision of Eastern and Western cultures creates a tapestry of captivating beauty and wonder. Nestled at the confluence of Europe and Asia, Istanbul is a city steeped in history, adorned with architectural marvels, and brimming with cultural diversity that has enticed travelers for generations. From its iconic landmarks to its bustling markets and delectable cuisine, Istanbul beckons adventurous souls to delve into its heart and soul, uncovering treasures at every turn.

As you embark on your voyage through Istanbul, let this comprehensive travel guide be your trusted companion, offering insider insights, top attractions, and hidden gems to ensure your journey is nothing short of extraordinary. Whether you're a history aficionado eager to delve into ancient ruins and Byzantine relics or a gastronome yearning for the flavors of authentic Turkish fare, Istanbul promises an experience like no other, inviting you to immerse yourself in a realm of discovery and adventure.

Istanbul: A Fusion of Cultures and Histories
Istanbul stands as a testament to the melding of diverse cultures and rich histories, bearing the imprints of empires past while embracing the vibrancy of contemporary life. With its strategic

location straddling two continents, Istanbul has served as the capital of multiple empires, including the Byzantine, Roman, and Ottoman, each leaving behind a legacy of architectural splendor and cultural heritage.

Begin your exploration of Istanbul's illustrious past at the iconic Hagia Sophia, a UNESCO World Heritage Site that has witnessed the ebb and flow of empires for over a millennium. Marvel at its soaring dome, intricate mosaics, and awe-inspiring architecture, reflecting the city's Byzantine roots and Ottoman influence.

Journey through time as you wander the labyrinthine corridors of the Topkapi Palace, once the opulent residence of Ottoman sultans and now a museum showcasing exquisite artifacts, imperial treasures, and stunning views of the Bosphorus. Delve into the intricate designs of the Blue Mosque, adorned with dazzling blue tiles and graceful minarets, offering a serene sanctuary amidst the bustling streets of Istanbul.

Explore the remnants of ancient civilizations at the Roman Hippodrome, where chariot races once thrilled the masses, and the hauntingly beautiful Basilica Cistern, an underground reservoir adorned with mysterious Medusa heads and ethereal lighting. With each step, you'll uncover layers of history and culture that have shaped Istanbul into the vibrant tapestry it is today.

Savoring the Flavors of Istanbul

No journey through Istanbul would be complete without indulging in its tantalizing cuisine, a melting pot of flavors and influences that reflects the city's diverse cultural heritage. From savory street food to sumptuous meze platters, Istanbul offers a culinary adventure like no other, tempting taste buds and igniting the senses with every bite.

Start your culinary odyssey with a visit to the bustling Spice Bazaar, where the vibrant hues and fragrant aromas of exotic spices, dried fruits, and Turkish delights beckon visitors to sample their wares. Take a stroll along the bustling streets of Kadikoy or Karakoy, where street vendors dish out delectable treats such as simit (sesame bread rings), grilled fish sandwiches, and succulent kebabs, providing a taste of Istanbul's vibrant street food scene.

For a more refined dining experience, venture into the historic neighborhoods of Sultanahmet or Beyoglu, where traditional meyhane and lokantas serve up an array of mouthwatering mezes, grilled meats, and hearty stews. Sample signature dishes like kofte (spiced meatballs), imam bayildi (stuffed eggplant), and baklava (sweet pastry) while sipping on refreshing glasses of Turkish tea or raki, the anise-flavored spirit that is synonymous with Turkish hospitality.

As the sun sets over the Bosphorus, indulge in a memorable dining experience at one of Istanbul's waterfront restaurants, where panoramic views and fresh seafood await. Feast on grilled octopus, meze platters, and freshly caught fish while basking in the warm glow of the city lights, savoring every moment of your culinary journey through Istanbul.

Off-the-Beaten-Path Adventures
While Istanbul's iconic landmarks and bustling bazaars may steal the spotlight, the city is also home to a myriad of off-the-beaten-path adventures waiting to be discovered by intrepid travelers. Escape the crowds and venture into the lesser-known corners of Istanbul, where hidden gems and secret treasures await.

Embark on a leisurely cruise along the tranquil waters of the Golden Horn, where historic neighborhoods and ancient fortifications unfold before your eyes. Discover hidden passages and hidden courtyards in the labyrinthine streets of Balat and Fener, two of Istanbul's most charming and atmospheric districts, where colorful houses, quaint cafes, and local artisans beckon visitors to explore.

Uncover the mysteries of Istanbul's lesser-known monuments and landmarks, such as the Chora Church, renowned for its dazzling mosaics and frescoes, or the Rumeli Hisari, a fortress perched atop a hill overlooking the Bosphorus, offering panoramic views of the city below. Wander through tranquil parks and verdant gardens, where locals gather to picnic, relax, and soak in the beauty of nature amidst the urban sprawl.

For a taste of traditional Turkish culture, immerse yourself in the vibrant rhythms and colorful costumes of a folk dance performance or attend a traditional Turkish bath ceremony, where centuries-old rituals and customs are preserved and celebrated. From hidden cafes and underground galleries to secret gardens and rooftop bars, Istanbul's off-the-beaten-path adventures promise unforgettable experiences and memories that will last a lifetime.

Let's Continue..

Chapter 1

ESSENTIAL PLANNING

Preparing For Your Trip

Embarking on a journey to Istanbul necessitates careful preparation to ensure a seamless and enriching experience in this dynamic city. This chapter serves as your guide, offering practical insights and valuable suggestions to streamline your planning process effectively.

1. Researching Istanbul: Immerse yourself in the cultural tapestry of Istanbul by delving into its history, customs, and renowned attractions. Familiarize yourself with iconic landmarks, local traditions, and essential Turkish phrases. This foundational knowledge will deepen your connection to Istanbul's heritage and enhance the gratification of your exploration.

2. Visa Requirements and Entry Procedures: Navigate the intricacies of entry into Istanbul by acquainting yourself with visa prerequisites tailored to your nationality. While some travelers can procure a tourist visa upon arrival, others may need to secure one beforehand. Ensure your passport

complies with validity criteria and any additional entry stipulations.

3. Packing Essentials: Tailor your packing list to suit Istanbul's climate and planned activities. Consider packing comfortable footwear for extensive walking, lightweight attire for warm summers, versatile layers for cooler evenings, sun protection essentials, a refillable water receptacle for hydration, and a universal adapter for electronic devices.

4. Travel Insurance: Mitigate unforeseen risks associated with travel by investing in comprehensive travel insurance. Safeguard against potential setbacks like flight disruptions, medical emergencies, or luggage misplacement by selecting a policy offering robust coverage for medical expenses, trip interruptions, and personal belongings.

5. Health and Safety Precautions: Prioritize your well-being by consulting with medical professionals or travel health experts before departure. Stay abreast of recommended vaccinations and preemptive health measures to safeguard against prevalent travel-related ailments. Familiarize yourself with emergency protocols and local medical resources in Istanbul.

6. Money Matters: Navigate Istanbul's financial landscape by acquainting yourself with the local currency, Turkish Lira (TRY). Consider exchanging currency beforehand to streamline transactions upon arrival. Notify your financial institution of your travel itinerary to preempt any potential card usage disruptions. Exercise prudence when accessing ATMs and exercise discretion with cash handling.

7. Communication and Connectivity: Ensure seamless communication throughout your Istanbul sojourn by procuring a reliable means of connectivity. Whether through a local SIM card, international roaming package, or internet-based messaging platforms, prioritize staying connected. Familiarize yourself with basic Turkish phrases to foster meaningful interactions and enrich your cultural immersion.

By meticulously preparing for your Istanbul excursion, you pave the way for a gratifying and hassle-free journey. Arm yourself with knowledge, plan thoughtfully, and approach your adventure with enthusiasm. With diligent preparation, you're poised to embark on an unforgettable odyssey through the captivating streets of Istanbul.

Visa Requirements And Entry Procedures

When planning your journey to Istanbul, comprehending the visa prerequisites and entry procedures is paramount to facilitate a seamless arrival and entry into Turkey. Here's an exhaustive guide to steer you through this pivotal aspect of your travel arrangements:

1. Visa Requirements:
- Visa-Free Travel: Numerous countries, including those within the Schengen Area, the United States, Canada, and Australia, allow their citizens visa-free entry to Turkey for short stays. However, the duration of permissible stays varies, ranging from 30 to 90 days within a 180-day timeframe, contingent upon nationality.

- Electronic Visa (e-Visa): For travelers from non-visa-free countries, Turkey provides an electronic visa (e-Visa) system, enabling online visa applications prior to departure. Typically valid for multiple entries, the e-Visa grants stays of up to 90 days within a 180-day period. The application process is user-friendly and can be accessed via the official Turkish government website.

- Visa on Arrival: Certain nationalities qualify for visa on arrival at Turkish airports and border checkpoints. Nonetheless, it's imperative to verify the latest eligibility criteria and prerequisites for visa on arrival, as regulations may undergo revisions.

2. Application Process:

- e-Visa Application: Prospective e-Visa applicants must complete an online form, furnishing personal particulars, passport information, and travel details. Payment of the e-Visa fee is securely transacted online using a credit or debit card. Upon approval, the e-Visa is dispatched to the applicant via email, to be either printed or saved digitally for presentation upon arrival in Turkey.

- Visa on Arrival: Eligible travelers seeking a visa on arrival must ensure compliance with all stipulations, including possession of a valid passport, requisite documentation (such as proof of lodging and onward travel), and adequate financial means for the duration of their stay. Visa fees are typically settled in local currency, payable in cash upon arrival.

3. Passport Requirements:

- Confirm that your passport remains valid for at least six months beyond your intended departure date from Turkey.

- Verify that your passport contains adequate blank pages for entry and exit endorsements.

4. Entry Procedures:

- Upon reaching Istanbul, proceed to the immigration counters with your passport, visa (if applicable), and supporting paperwork.
- Submit your documents to the immigration officer for authentication and issuance of entry stamps.
- Retain your arrival card, possibly distributed during your flight, as it will be necessary upon exiting Turkey.

5. Extension and Overstay Penalties:
- Travelers intending to prolong their stay in Turkey beyond the authorized visa or visa-free duration must petition for an extension through local immigration authorities.
- Overstaying sanctioned timeframes may lead to penalties, deportation, or prohibition from reentry, underscoring the importance of adhering to approved lengths of stay.

Acquiring a comprehensive understanding of visa prerequisites and entry procedures is pivotal for a seamless travel venture to Istanbul. By acquainting yourself with pertinent visa regulations, completing requisite application procedures, and ensuring conformity with entry requisites, you can embark on your Istanbul odyssey with assurance and anticipation.

Best Time To Visit Istanbul

Istanbul, a city steeped in history, adorned with breathtaking architecture, and pulsating with cultural vibrancy, extends a year-round invitation to travelers. However, selecting the opportune moment to explore can significantly elevate your sojourn. Delve into the seasonal nuances and climatic patterns to tailor your trip in alignment with your preferences and pursuits.

Spring:

April through June heralds springtime, arguably Istanbul's pinnacle. The weather graces with mildness, accompanied by blooming flora adorning parks and gardens. Embrace outdoor escapades, delve into sightseeing, and traverse historical marvels sans the sweltering summer heat or the throngs of peak tourism.

Summer:

From June to August, summer envelopes Istanbul in warmth and azure skies. While elongated daylight hours beckon leisurely strolls along the Bosphorus and idyllic cafe reveries, it also heralds peak tourist influx. Brace for bustling crowds at landmarks and elevated accommodation rates. Yet, amidst the fervor, summer pulsates with vivacity, hosting myriad festivals and events citywide.

Autumn:

September to November casts Istanbul in a tranquil allure, offering a reprieve from summer's hustle. Temperatures taper to comfortable levels, ideal for exploring open-air attractions and architectural gems. As foliage dons autumnal hues, Istanbul unveils its picturesque charm, casting a captivating spell over your sojourn.

Winter:

December through February ushers in winter's embrace, accompanied by cooler climes and sporadic showers. While some may shy away, winter exudes a distinct allure, beckoning with diminished crowds and pocket-friendly accommodation rates. Revel in indoor pursuits like museum perusing, gallery hopping, and indulging in traditional Turkish baths. Moreover, immerse yourself in the festive fervor of the season, with Christmas markets and New Year's festivities adding a touch of enchantment to your experience.

Ultimately, the choice of when to explore Istanbul hinges on personal inclinations, financial considerations, and travel aspirations. Whether reveling in spring's gentleness, basking in summer's exuberance, savoring autumn's tranquility, or embracing winter's coziness, Istanbul extends a warm embrace year-round. Armed with insights into seasonal fluctuations, chart your course with confidence, and prepare for an unforgettable journey in this mesmerizing metropolis.

Now, equipped with the knowledge of Istanbul's optimal times to visit, let's embark on crafting your itinerary with sampled schedules tailored to diverse durations and interests.

Chapter 2

PLANNING THE TRIP:
SAMPLED ITINERARIES

One Week in Istanbul: A Comprehensive Itineraries

Congratulations on choosing Istanbul as your destination for a week-long adventure! With its blend of history, culture, and culinary delights, Istanbul promises an unforgettable experience. This comprehensive itinerary will guide you through the must-see attractions, hidden gems, and immersive experiences that make Istanbul a truly remarkable city.

Day 1: Arrival and Old City Exploration
- Morning: Arrive in Istanbul and check into your accommodation in the Sultanahmet area, ideally situated for exploring the city's historic heart.
- Afternoon: Begin your journey with a visit to the iconic Hagia Sophia, a marvel of Byzantine architecture. Explore its stunning interior adorned with intricate mosaics and learn about its fascinating history.
- Evening: Continue your exploration with a stroll to the nearby Blue Mosque, famous for its striking blue tiles and towering minarets. Take in the serene

atmosphere as the call to prayer echoes through the courtyard at sunset. End the day with a leisurely dinner at a traditional Turkish restaurant, savoring delicious mezes and kebabs.

Day 2: Topkapi Palace and Grand Bazaar
- Morning: Spend the morning exploring Topkapi Palace, the former residence of Ottoman sultans. Wander through its opulent chambers, admire the dazzling treasures of the Imperial Treasury, and enjoy panoramic views of the Bosphorus from the palace grounds.
- Afternoon: Head to the bustling Grand Bazaar, one of the world's oldest and largest covered markets. Get lost in its labyrinthine alleys lined with shops selling everything from spices and textiles to jewelry and ceramics. Don't forget to haggle for souvenirs and indulge in some Turkish delight.
- Evening: Relax with a scenic Bosphorus cruise, sailing past historic landmarks and picturesque neighborhoods illuminated against the night sky. Enjoy dinner at a waterfront restaurant, sampling fresh seafood and watching the twinkling lights of the cityscape.

Day 3: Bosphorus Exploration and Spice Bazaar
- Morning: Embark on a guided cruise along the Bosphorus, the strait that divides Europe and Asia. Admire the city's skyline from the water, passing

under majestic bridges and alongside Ottoman palaces. Learn about Istanbul's rich maritime history and soak in the beauty of its waterfront mansions.
- Afternoon: Disembark at the Spice Bazaar, a sensory delight filled with exotic spices, dried fruits, and Turkish sweets. Take your time browsing the stalls and sampling local delicacies like Turkish delight and baklava. Don't miss the chance to sip traditional Turkish tea at a charming tea house.
- Evening: Explore the vibrant neighborhoods of Beyoglu and Karakoy, known for their trendy cafes, art galleries, and nightlife. Stroll down Istiklal Avenue, Istanbul's bustling pedestrian street, and immerse yourself in the city's contemporary culture.

Day 4: Asian Side and Kadikoy Market
- Morning: Cross the Bosphorus to the Asian side of Istanbul and explore the lively neighborhood of Kadikoy. Wander through its bustling streets lined with colorful shops, cafes, and street vendors. Visit the Kadikoy Market to sample fresh produce, local cheeses, and olives.
- Afternoon: Take a leisurely walk along the Kadikoy waterfront promenade, enjoying panoramic views of the Bosphorus and Istanbul's European skyline. Stop for a traditional Turkish lunch at a local meyhane, where you can feast on mezes, grilled fish, and Turkish raki.

- Evening: Return to the European side and spend the evening in the vibrant neighborhood of Ortakoy. Admire the ornate Ortakoy Mosque and stroll along the waterfront, where vendors sell street food and handmade crafts. Enjoy dinner at one of the waterfront restaurants, soaking in the lively atmosphere.

Day 5: Day Trip to Princes' Islands
- Morning: Escape the hustle and bustle of the city with a day trip to the Princes' Islands, a group of nine car-free islands in the Sea of Marmara. Take a ferry from Kabatas or Bostanci and enjoy the scenic journey to the largest island, Buyukada.
- Afternoon: Explore Buyukada's charming streets lined with wooden Ottoman mansions and lush gardens. Rent a bicycle or horse-drawn carriage to explore the island at a leisurely pace. Visit the historic Aya Yorgi Monastery perched atop a hill for panoramic views of the island and the sea.
- Evening: Indulge in a seafood dinner at one of Buyukada's waterfront restaurants, enjoying freshly caught fish and seafood delicacies. Take the ferry back to Istanbul as the sun sets over the Marmara Sea, ending your day with a memorable sunset cruise.

Day 6: Cultural Immersion and Culinary Delights

- Morning: Start your day with a visit to the Istanbul Modern Museum, Turkey's premier contemporary art museum. Explore its diverse collection of Turkish and international art, housed in a former warehouse overlooking the Bosphorus.
- Afternoon: Immerse yourself in Turkish culture with a visit to a traditional hammam, where you can indulge in a relaxing bath and invigorating massage. Alternatively, take a cooking class and learn to prepare classic Turkish dishes like dolma, kebabs, and baklava.
- Evening: Experience Istanbul's vibrant nightlife with dinner and drinks in the lively neighborhood of Beyoglu. Explore its eclectic mix of bars, cafes, and live music venues, and mingle with locals and fellow travelers alike.

Day 7: Farewell and Departure
- Morning: Spend your final morning in Istanbul exploring any remaining sights or neighborhoods on your bucket list. Visit a local market to pick up last-minute souvenirs or gifts for loved ones back home.
- Afternoon: Check out of your accommodation and transfer to the airport for your departure. Reflect on your unforgettable week in Istanbul and cherish the memories you've made in this captivating city.

As you journey through Istanbul, may this comprehensive itinerary serve as a roadmap for your adventures and discoveries. Whether you're marveling at historic landmarks, savoring local delicacies, or immersing yourself in Turkish culture, may each moment be filled with joy, wonder, and unforgettable experiences.

Weekend Getaway: Making The Most Of Two Days

While two days may seem short, this itinerary is carefully crafted to help you make the most of your time in this enchanting city.

Day 1: Arrival and Old City Exploration
- Morning: Arrive in Istanbul and kick off your weekend adventure by checking into your accommodation in the Sultanahmet area, ideally located for exploring the city's historic landmarks.
- Afternoon: Start your exploration with a visit to the iconic Hagia Sophia, a masterpiece of Byzantine architecture. Marvel at its grandeur as you explore its intricate mosaics and learn about its rich history.
- Evening: Continue your journey with a visit to the Blue Mosque, known for its stunning blue tiles and graceful minarets. Take a leisurely stroll through Sultanahmet Square and soak in the ambiance of this historic neighborhood. End the day with a delicious dinner at a local restaurant, sampling traditional Turkish dishes like kebabs and mezes.

Day 2: Bosphorus Cruise and Spice Bazaar

- Morning: Begin your day with a scenic Bosphorus cruise, offering panoramic views of Istanbul's skyline and waterfront landmarks. Sail past historic palaces, mosques, and bridges while learning about the city's maritime heritage.

- Afternoon: Disembark at the Spice Bazaar, a bustling marketplace filled with exotic spices, dried fruits, and Turkish sweets. Take your time exploring the maze of stalls and indulging in tastings of local delicacies like Turkish delight and baklava.

- Evening: Conclude your weekend getaway with a visit to the vibrant neighborhood of Karakoy. Explore its trendy cafes, boutiques, and art galleries, soaking in the bohemian atmosphere. Treat yourself to dinner at a waterfront restaurant, enjoying panoramic views of the Bosphorus as you savor delicious seafood dishes.

This weekend itinerary offers a taste of Istanbul's rich history, vibrant culture, and culinary delights, ensuring a memorable and fulfilling getaway. Whether you're exploring ancient landmarks, cruising along the Bosphorus, or savoring Turkish flavors, may your weekend in Istanbul be filled with adventure, discovery, and unforgettable experiences.

Off The Beaten Path: Alternatives Experiences In Istanbul

While Istanbul's iconic landmarks and bustling bazaars draw millions of visitors each year, the city also offers a wealth of off-the-beaten-path experiences waiting to be discovered. This itinerary is designed for adventurous travelers seeking unique and unconventional ways to explore Istanbul's hidden gems.

Day 1: Urban Exploration and Street Art
- Morning: Start your day with a visit to Karakoy, a vibrant neighborhood known for its artistic flair and bohemian atmosphere. Wander through its maze of narrow streets lined with colorful street art, graffiti, and murals, created by local and international artists.
- Afternoon: Dive deeper into Istanbul's urban art scene with a guided street art tour, led by a knowledgeable local guide. Discover hidden gems tucked away in back alleys and abandoned buildings, and learn about the cultural and social significance of street art in Istanbul.
- Evening: Wrap up your day with a visit to an underground art gallery or alternative cultural space, showcasing the works of emerging artists and experimental performers. Immerse yourself in

Istanbul's creative scene, mingling with artists and fellow travelers alike.

Day 2: Nature Retreat and Local Communities
- Morning: Escape the hustle and bustle of the city with a day trip to Belgrade Forest, a peaceful oasis located on the outskirts of Istanbul. Hike along scenic trails, breathe in the fresh air, and immerse yourself in the tranquility of nature.
- Afternoon: Explore Istanbul's lesser-known neighborhoods and local communities, where traditional ways of life and cultural heritage thrive. Visit neighborhoods like Balat and Fener, known for their historic architecture, colorful houses, and vibrant street life.
- Evening: Experience Istanbul's culinary diversity with a visit to a local market or food bazaar, where you can sample authentic Turkish dishes and regional specialties. Engage with local vendors, learn about traditional cooking techniques, and savor the flavors of Istanbul's diverse culinary landscape.

Day 3: Spiritual Exploration and Healing
- Morning: Begin your day with a visit to one of Istanbul's lesser-known mosques or spiritual retreats, where you can immerse yourself in quiet contemplation and reflection. Seek out hidden gems like the Rustem Pasha Mosque or the Sufi dervish

lodges, where you can experience the mystical traditions of Islam.

- Afternoon: Indulge in a rejuvenating spa experience at one of Istanbul's traditional hammams or Turkish baths. Treat yourself to a relaxing bath, followed by a therapeutic massage and exfoliating scrub, leaving you feeling refreshed and revitalized.

- Evening: Conclude your off-the-beaten-path adventure with a sunset meditation session or yoga class, held in a serene outdoor setting overlooking the Bosphorus or the city skyline. Reflect on your journey through Istanbul's alternative experiences, and embrace the sense of peace and harmony that surrounds you.

This off-the-beaten-path itinerary offers a unique perspective on Istanbul, allowing you to discover hidden treasures, connect with local communities, and embark on transformative experiences. Whether you're exploring urban art, communing with nature, or seeking spiritual renewal, may your journey through Istanbul be filled with discovery, wonder, and meaningful connections. Safe travels and enjoy your off-the-beaten-path adventure in this fascinating city!

Chapter 3

ICONIC LANDMARKS AND MUST-SEE ATTRACTION

Hagia Sophia: A Marvel Of Byzantine Architecture

Hagia Sophia, an epitome of Byzantine architecture, enthralls visitors with its majestic dome, intricate mosaics, and rich history. Originally constructed as a Christian basilica, later repurposed as a mosque, and now serving as a museum, Hagia Sophia symbolizes Istanbul's cultural richness and architectural brilliance.

Emperor Justinian I commissioned Hagia Sophia in the 6th century to rival Rome's St. Peter's Basilica. Crafted by architects Anthemius of Tralles and Isidore of Miletus, its innovative design, highlighted by a colossal dome and detailed mosaics, set new benchmarks in Byzantine architecture.

Across centuries, Hagia Sophia underwent transformations mirroring Istanbul's evolving religious and political landscape. Post the Ottoman conquest in 1453, it morphed into a mosque with added minarets, symbolizing the city's Muslim identity. Secularized in 1935 by the Republic of

Turkey, it became a museum, allowing diverse audiences to admire its splendor. However, its recent reversion to a mosque in July 2020 reignited debates on its identity and significance.

Architecture:
Hagia Sophia's architectural marvel lies in its innovative design and engineering prowess. Its colossal dome, spanning 31 meters in diameter and rising 55 meters above ground, supported by pendentives and semi-domes, evokes awe and majesty.

The interior dazzles with intricate mosaics, marble columns, and ornate decorations, showcasing Byzantine artisans' skill. Iconic religious scenes adorn the walls, depicting Christ, the Virgin Mary, and saints with vivid detail and vibrant colors.

Externally, a fusion of Byzantine and Ottoman styles is evident, with towering minarets, elaborate portals, and intricate stone carvings. This dual identity reflects Istanbul's multicultural heritage.

Legacy:
Hagia Sophia transcends architectural significance, embodying Istanbul's complex history and cultural fabric. As a UNESCO World Heritage Site, it draws

millions annually, captivated by its beauty and spiritual resonance.

Despite controversies, Hagia Sophia remains a beacon of resilience and cultural dialogue, bridging East and West, Christianity and Islam. It stands as a testament to human creativity and architectural prowess, inspiring wonder and admiration across generations.

Blue Mosque: A Symbol Of Istanbul's Skyline

Gracing the skyline of Istanbul with its six minarets and stunning blue tiles, the Blue Mosque, also known as Sultan Ahmed Mosque, stands as a magnificent testament to the city's rich cultural heritage and architectural splendor. Admired for its elegant design, intricate decorations, and spiritual significance, the Blue Mosque holds a special place in the hearts of both locals and visitors alike.

Commissioned by Sultan Ahmed I in the early 17th century, the Blue Mosque was constructed to rival the grandeur of Hagia Sophia, located just a stone's throw away. Designed by the renowned architect Mehmet Aga, the mosque was envisioned as a symbol of Ottoman power and piety, showcasing the empire's architectural prowess and religious devotion.

Construction of the Blue Mosque began in 1609 and was completed in 1616, spanning seven years of meticulous craftsmanship and labor. The mosque's name, "Blue Mosque," is derived from the thousands of blue tiles adorning its interior, creating a mesmerizing sea of color that bathes the prayer hall in a tranquil blue light.

The Blue Mosque's architectural style blends elements of classical Ottoman design with influences from Byzantine and Islamic traditions. Its expansive courtyard, adorned with marble fountains and surrounded by arched colonnades, welcomes visitors into a sanctuary of peace and serenity.

The mosque's exterior is adorned with intricate stone carvings, cascading domes, and towering minarets, creating a silhouette that dominates the Istanbul skyline. The central dome, rising to a height of 43 meters, is flanked by four smaller domes and supported by slender columns and semi-domes, creating a harmonious balance of light and space.

Inside, the Blue Mosque dazzles visitors with its breathtaking beauty and architectural symmetry. The vast prayer hall, illuminated by the soft glow of stained glass windows and intricate chandeliers, is adorned with delicate floral motifs, geometric patterns, and calligraphic inscriptions, all meticulously crafted by skilled artisans.

As one of Istanbul's most beloved landmarks, the Blue Mosque holds a special place in the hearts of locals and visitors alike. Beyond its architectural significance, the mosque serves as a center of religious devotion and spiritual contemplation, welcoming worshippers from around the world to pray and reflect in its hallowed halls.

Throughout its storied history, the Blue Mosque has weathered wars, earthquakes, and political upheavals, yet it remains a symbol of resilience and faith. Today, as visitors marvel at its beauty and significance, they are reminded of the enduring power of architecture to inspire awe, reverence, and a sense of connection to something greater than themselves.

Whether bathed in the soft light of dawn or illuminated against the night sky, the Blue Mosque continues to captivate and inspire, inviting all who enter its sacred space to experience a moment of peace, beauty, and transcendence amidst the bustling streets of Istanbul.

Topkapi Palace: Home To Ottoman Sultans

Nestled atop the historic peninsula of Istanbul, Topkapi Palace stands as a majestic symbol of the Ottoman Empire's grandeur and opulence. For centuries, it served as the political and administrative center of the empire, housing generations of Ottoman sultans and their court. Today, Topkapi Palace is a UNESCO World Heritage Site and one of Istanbul's most visited attractions, offering visitors a glimpse into the lavish lifestyle and rich cultural heritage of the Ottoman era.

Topkapi Palace has a rich and storied history that spans over four centuries, from its construction in the 15th century to its transformation into a museum in the 20th century. Commissioned by Sultan Mehmed the Conqueror in 1459, the palace was initially built as a royal residence and administrative center for the burgeoning Ottoman Empire.

Over the centuries, successive sultans expanded and renovated Topkapi Palace, adding new wings, courtyards, and pavilions to accommodate the growing needs of the imperial court. The palace became not only a seat of political power but also a center of artistic patronage, with artisans and craftsmen creating exquisite works of art and craftsmanship to adorn its halls and chambers.

Following the decline of the Ottoman Empire in the 19th century, Topkapi Palace fell into disrepair and neglect. However, in the early 20th century, efforts were made to restore and preserve the palace as a museum, allowing visitors to explore its rich history and cultural treasures.

The architecture of Topkapi Palace reflects a blend of Byzantine, Persian, and Islamic influences, with its sprawling complex of courtyards, gardens, and pavilions showcasing the finest examples of Ottoman architectural design.

The palace is organized into a series of interconnected courtyards, each serving a specific function within the imperial complex. The First Courtyard, known as the Court of the Janissaries, was once the domain of the elite Janissary corps and now houses the Hagia Irene Church and various exhibition spaces.

Moving deeper into the palace, visitors enter the Second Courtyard, home to the Divan, or council chamber, where state affairs were conducted. Nearby, the Imperial Council Chamber and the Tower of Justice stand as reminders of the palace's role as the seat of Ottoman governance.

The Third Courtyard, also known as the Inner Palace, is the heart of Topkapi Palace, housing the private quarters of the sultan and his family. Here, visitors can explore the opulent apartments of the sultan, including the Imperial Harem, where the sultan's wives, concubines, and children resided.

As one of Istanbul's most iconic landmarks, Topkapi Palace stands as a testament to the grandeur and legacy of the Ottoman Empire. Beyond its architectural significance, the palace is a treasure trove of cultural artifacts, including priceless manuscripts, ceramics, and textiles, that offer insight into the art, history, and daily life of the Ottoman court.

Today, visitors to Topkapi Palace can explore its vast halls and chambers, marvel at its exquisite architecture and craftsmanship, and immerse themselves in the rich tapestry of Ottoman history and culture. From the glittering treasures of the Imperial Treasury to the serene beauty of the palace gardens, Topkapi Palace continues to captivate and inspire, inviting visitors on a journey through the splendor of the Ottoman era.

Grand Bazaar: A Treasure Trove of Turkish Delights

Nestled in the vibrant heart of Istanbul, the Grand Bazaar stands tall, a testament to the city's enduring legacy, cultural richness, and entrepreneurial fervor. Its winding alleys, bustling stalls, and centuries-old customs beckon visitors into a world of sensory delights, establishing it as a cherished and emblematic landmark of Istanbul.

Dating back to the 15th century, the Grand Bazaar owes its inception to the vision of Mehmed the Conqueror, who sought to invigorate trade and commerce in the burgeoning Ottoman capital. What commenced as a modest marketplace swiftly burgeoned into a sprawling complex of domes, courtyards, and caravanserais, drawing in traders and merchants from far-flung corners of the Ottoman Empire and beyond.

Over the ages, the Grand Bazaar metamorphosed, mirroring Istanbul's evolving economic and cultural fabric. Under the patronage of successive sultans, it blossomed into a nexus of commerce, craftsmanship, and cultural intermingling, with artisans and merchants honing their expertise in an array of goods, from textiles and ceramics to spices and jewels.

Today, the Grand Bazaar remains a behemoth of trade, spanning over 61 streets and hosting myriad shops, boutiques, and stalls. Its enduring allure continues to captivate millions annually, offering an unparalleled amalgamation of tradition, commerce, and culture.

The architectural ensemble of the Grand Bazaar narrates a saga of opulence and diversity, with its labyrinthine design, soaring domes, and intricate embellishments epitomizing the splendor of Ottoman aesthetics.

Structured as a labyrinth of interconnected streets, alleys, and courtyards, each precinct specializes in distinct merchandise. From the clamor of the Jewelry Bazaar to the fragrant allure of the Spice Market, visitors embark on a sensory odyssey, navigating through a kaleidoscope of hues, textures, and fragrances.

At its core lies the Cevahir Bedesten, or "Inner Bedesten," an erstwhile stronghold safeguarding the most prized commodities like gold, silver, and gemstones. Today, it serves as the sanctuary of the bazaar's esteemed purveyors and craftsmen, showcasing an array of exquisite jewelry, handwoven carpets, and other marvels of Turkish artistry.

The Grand Bazaar occupies an indelible niche in the collective consciousness of Istanbul's denizens and tourists alike. Beyond its commercial prominence, it stands as a bastion of culture, preserving age-old traditions and crafts integral to Turkey's cultural mosaic.

For centuries, the Grand Bazaar has served as a melting pot of diversity and cosmopolitanism, uniting individuals from varied creeds, backgrounds, and cultures. Even today, it remains a hallowed ground where East intersects West, where ancient customs coalesce with contemporary commerce, fostering a vibrant tapestry of encounters and experiences.

More than a mere marketplace, the Grand Bazaar is an immersive cultural voyage, wherein visitors bear witness to the ingenuity of Turkish artisans, engage in spirited barter with merchants, and revel in the ambiance of one of the world's most storied marketplaces.

As you traverse its bustling bylanes and hidden recesses, may the Grand Bazaar unfurl its enchantment before you, weaving a tapestry of delight, wonder, and indelible reminiscences.

Bosphorus Cruise: Sailing Between Two Continents

Dividing the bustling city of Istanbul, the Bosphorus Strait emerges as a natural marvel bridging two continents: Europe and Asia. Embarking on a Bosphorus cruise unveils an enchanting voyage along this historic waterway, where panoramic vistas, ancient landmarks, and vibrant neighborhoods converge to narrate the rich cultural tapestry of Istanbul.

For millennia, the Bosphorus Strait has woven itself into the fabric of Istanbul's history and identity. Serving as a crucial maritime artery connecting the Black Sea to the Mediterranean, it has facilitated trade, commerce, and cultural dialogue between Europe and Asia since antiquity.

Across epochs, the Bosphorus has stood witness to the ebb and flow of empires, the march of armies, and the migratory movements of peoples. Immortalized in literature, poetry, and art, it embodies Istanbul's allure, romance, and mystique.

Presently, the Bosphorus remains integral to Istanbul's transportation network, teeming with ferries, cargo vessels, and pleasure boats traversing its waters day and night. A Bosphorus cruise offers a firsthand encounter with this iconic waterway, providing an unparalleled perspective on the city's topography, architecture, and heritage.

A Bosphorus cruise unfolds as a sensory extravaganza, treating passengers to spellbinding vistas of Istanbul's skyline, historic edifices, and natural splendor. Drifting along the glistening expanse of the strait, one revels in panoramas of majestic palaces, ancient citadels, and verdant hillsides adorned with stately mansions.

Among the cruise's highlights is the chance to behold Istanbul's iconic landmarks from a fresh vantage point. Behold the soaring domes and minarets of Hagia Sophia and the Blue Mosque, commanding the cityscape. Admire the regal contours of Topkapi Palace and the formidable ramparts of Rumeli Fortress, sentinel to the Bosphorus entrance.

As the vessel glides past picturesque waterfront districts like Ortakoy, Bebek, and Arnavutkoy, passengers witness the vibrant tableau of Istanbul's shoreline life. From fishermen casting nets to families picnicking in shoreline parks, the Bosphorus unveils the rhythm of daily existence in this bustling metropolis.

The shores of the Bosphorus bear testament to Istanbul's architectural diversity and cultural legacy. Here, a medley of Ottoman palaces, waterfront mansions, and contemporary structures narrate the city's storied past and dynamic present.

Foremost among these architectural marvels is Dolmabahce Palace, an exemplar of Ottoman Baroque opulence that served as the imperial seat in the 19th century. With its resplendent facade, opulent interiors, and sprawling gardens, it offers a glimpse into the lavish lifestyle of Ottoman royalty.

Equally captivating is the Bosphorus Bridge, a modern engineering marvel spanning the strait to unite Europe and Asia. Passing beneath its soaring arches, passengers are awestruck by its monumental scale and graceful design, embodying Istanbul's ethos of modernity and progress.

Beyond its geographical significance, the Bosphorus stands as a cultural crossroads where East meets West, past intersects present. Along its banks, a rich tapestry of cultures, traditions, and communities unfolds, shaping Istanbul's identity across the ages.

From the ancient vestiges of Byzantium to the vibrant neighborhoods of contemporary Istanbul, the Bosphorus cruise unfolds as a voyage through time and space. Here, one delves into the city's layered history and multicultural heritage, whether marveling at Ottoman grandeur or savoring Turkish culinary delights in waterfront eateries.

Sailing between two continents aboard a Bosphorus cruise evokes the timeless allure and enduring relevance of this historic waterway. Whether a novice explorer or seasoned traveler, the Bosphorus promises an enchanting odyssey that lingers long after the journey concludes. So, recline and savor the sights and sounds of Istanbul's iconic thoroughfare as it guides you into the heart of this vivacious and captivating city.

Chapter 4

SPENDING WISELY

Budget-friendly Activities And Attractions

Embarking on an exploration of Istanbul need not strain your budget. With its storied history, dynamic culture, and diverse attractions, the city extends a plethora of budget-friendly options for travelers keen on maximizing their experience without overspending. From delving into historic landmarks to relishing local cuisine, Istanbul presents a multitude of affordable avenues for a fulfilling adventure. This chapter aims to spotlight some of the finest budget-friendly activities and attractions that Istanbul has in store, ensuring that you can revel in the city's allure without denting your wallet.

Immersing oneself in Istanbul's rich tapestry of history and culture often begins with a visit to its iconic landmarks, many of which are accessible to visitors at modest costs or even free of charge. Hagia Sophia, for instance, extends discounted admission tickets for students and seniors, rendering it an economical choice for budget-conscious travelers. Similarly, the Blue Mosque welcomes visitors without an entrance fee, enabling you to marvel at its architectural splendor and tranquil ambiance without spending a penny.

Another must-visit destination is the Topkapi Palace, erstwhile abode of the Ottoman sultans. While accessing the palace's main attractions may necessitate a ticket, its sprawling grounds and verdant gardens can be explored freely, allowing you to bask in the elegance of its architecture and savor panoramic vistas of the cityscape.

For those intrigued by Istanbul's ancient legacy, the Archaeological Museums beckon with an array of artifacts and exhibitions at a fraction of the cost charged by other museums in the city. From relics of ancient Greek and Roman civilizations to treasures from Byzantine and Ottoman eras, these museums proffer a captivating glimpse into Istanbul's bygone epochs without straining your budget.

Istanbul stands as a melting pot of cultures, and there's no better way to immerse oneself in its kaleidoscopic diversity than by delving into its vibrant cultural milieu. Fortunately, many cultural attractions and experiences in Istanbul are budget-friendly or even complimentary.

One such experience entails a foray into the city's bustling markets and bazaars, where you can sample local delicacies, negotiate for souvenirs, and absorb the sights and sounds of everyday life in Istanbul. The Grand Bazaar, a labyrinthine maze of narrow lanes and bustling stalls, offers a sensorial extravaganza of colors, aromas, and flavors that won't strain your budget.

Another budget-friendly cultural immersion involves attending traditional Turkish performances, such as whirling dervish ceremonies or folk music concerts. Held in historic venues or open-air settings, these performances typically offer affordable ticket prices, enabling you to savor a slice of Turkish culture without emptying your pockets.

For nature enthusiasts, Istanbul unfurls a tapestry of budget-friendly outdoor pursuits and verdant sanctuaries waiting to be explored. From scenic waterfront promenades to expansive parks and gardens, the city offers myriad opportunities to relish its natural splendor without incurring hefty expenses.

The Bosphorus waterfront emerges as a favored outdoor destination, inviting leisurely strolls along its shores, idyllic picnics in waterfront parks, or tranquil moments admiring the passing boats. Many of these activities come at no cost or entail nominal fees for amenities like picnic tables or bicycle rentals.

Similarly, embarking on a hike or walk along one of Istanbul's scenic trails or nature reserves promises an invigorating escape into nature without straining your budget. The Belgrade Forest, for instance, boasts miles of hiking trails winding through lush woodlands and babbling streams, offering a serene retreat from the city's hustle and bustle without necessitating a financial outlay.

A sojourn in Istanbul would be incomplete without savoring its renowned culinary offerings, and thankfully, there is no shortage of budget-friendly options for gastronomes on a tight budget. From street food vendors and local eateries to traditional markets and culinary tours, Istanbul's culinary landscape caters to every palate and budget.

Exploring Istanbul's street food scene stands out as one of the best ways to sample its diverse cuisine without breaking the bank. From savory kebabs and falafel wraps to indulgent pastries and desserts, the city's street food vendors proffer an enticing array of flavors at affordable prices.

For a deeper dive into Istanbul's culinary heritage, consider partaking in a food tour or cooking class, where you can delve into Turkish gastronomy, sample regional specialties, and even try your hand at preparing traditional dishes. Many of these experiences are reasonably priced and offer excellent value for money, allowing you to indulge in Istanbul's culinary delights without straining your budget.

When it comes to securing budget-friendly accommodations in Istanbul, the city abounds with options tailored to suit every traveler's preferences and financial constraints. From economical hotels and guesthouses to hostels and vacation rentals, there exists a plethora of affordable lodging choices that won't break the bank.

Hostels, in particular, emerge as a popular choice for budget-conscious travelers, offering affordable dormitory beds and communal facilities such as kitchens and common areas. Many hostels also organize social events and activities, fostering a convivial atmosphere ideal for solo travelers or those eager to forge new connections.

Alternatively, vacation rentals present another budget-friendly accommodation option in Istanbul, furnishing the comfort and convenience of a home away from home at a fraction of the cost of a hotel stay. Spanning from cozy studio apartments to spacious houses, vacation rentals cater to families or groups traveling together seeking value-oriented lodging.

Unraveling the wonders of Istanbul on a budget is not only feasible but also immensely rewarding, with a wealth of budget-friendly activities, attractions, and experiences awaiting exploration. Whether navigating historic landmarks, relishing local cuisine, or immersing oneself in the city's vibrant cultural milieu, Istanbul offers myriad opportunities to savor its allure without straining your finances.

By leveraging affordable accommodations, exploring complimentary or low-cost attractions, and seeking out budget-friendly dining options, you can partake in the magic of Istanbul without incurring exorbitant expenses. Thus, pack your bags, chart your itinerary, and prepare to bask in the sights, sounds, and flavors of this dynamic city on a budget-friendly escapade of a lifetime.

Tips For Bargaining At Markets And Souvenir Shops

Bargaining in Istanbul transcends mere transactional exchanges; it's a deeply rooted cultural tradition woven into the fabric of daily life. From the winding alleys of the Grand Bazaar to the quaint storefronts adorning Sultanahmet's streets, bargaining is an art form embraced by both locals and visitors alike. Mastering the nuances of negotiation not only saves you money but also offers profound insights into Turkish culture and customs. In this guide, we'll delve into essential tips for navigating markets and souvenir shops in Istanbul, empowering you to navigate the labyrinth of haggling with confidence and success.

1. Understanding the Cultural Context:
Before delving into the world of bargaining, it's imperative to grasp the cultural nuances that underpin this practice in Turkey. Bargaining isn't merely about securing the best price; it's about forging connections and establishing rapport with sellers. Approach bargaining with warmth and respect, fostering a friendly atmosphere that encourages meaningful dialogue and negotiation.

2. Commence with a Smile:
A genuine smile serves as a potent catalyst in the art of bargaining. Initiate the interaction with a

warm greeting and a heartfelt smile, signaling your openness to negotiation and goodwill. Establishing a positive rapport from the outset sets a congenial tone for the bargaining process and enhances the likelihood of striking a favorable deal.

3. Conduct Research:
In the realm of bargaining, knowledge is unequivocally power. Prior to embarking on your shopping excursion, conduct thorough research on the average prices of items you intend to purchase. Armed with this information, you'll possess a baseline for negotiations, enabling you to ascertain fair prices and make informed decisions. Websites, guidebooks, and travel forums serve as invaluable resources for gathering pricing insights in Istanbul.

4. Establish a Budget:
Before initiating negotiations, it's imperative to delineate a budget for your prospective purchases. Determine the maximum amount you're willing to spend and adhere to it steadfastly throughout the bargaining process. A predefined budget not only safeguards against overspending but also facilitates astute decision-making, ensuring optimal value for your expenditures.

5. Exercise Patience:

Bargaining demands patience and perseverance. Prepare to invest time and effort into negotiations, as fruitful outcomes often necessitate multiple rounds of discussion and compromise. Maintain composure and equanimity, even amid protracted or impassioned exchanges, as patience is a virtue that can yield favorable results.

6. Commence with a Low Offer:
Initiate negotiations by tendering an initial offer substantially lower than the seller's asking price. This strategic maneuver creates room for negotiation and enables incremental escalation of your bid while remaining within budgetary constraints. Starting low also conveys your seriousness about bargaining and underscores your resolve to secure a favorable deal.

7. Employ Politeness:
Courtesy and civility are indispensable currencies in the realm of bargaining. Employ polite language and respectful gestures when engaging with sellers, irrespective of negotiation outcomes. Refrain from adopting confrontational or aggressive stances, as such behavior undermines rapport and impedes productive discourse.

8. Know When to Walk Away:

Discerning when to gracefully exit negotiations can be an invaluable bargaining tactic. If dialogue reaches an impasse or sellers prove unwilling to meet your terms, gracefully express gratitude and depart in search of alternative vendors. The prospect of losing a potential sale may incentivize sellers to reconsider their stance and display greater flexibility.

9. Embrace Compromise:
Bargaining embodies a spirit of reciprocity, necessitating a willingness to compromise. Should sellers proffer counteroffers that align closely with your budget but slightly exceed your ideal price point, consider acquiescing if the deviation remains reasonable. Remember, bargaining is about arriving at mutually satisfactory terms that satisfy both parties.

10. Thoroughly Inspect Merchandise:
Before finalizing any transaction, meticulously examine the merchandise to assess its quality and condition. Scrutinize for defects, damages, or discrepancies that may influence its value or desirability. Leveraging any observed issues during negotiations empowers you to negotiate a lower price or request additional concessions.

11. Demonstrate Respect:

Above all, maintain a demeanor of respect and courtesy towards sellers throughout the bargaining process. Recognize that bargaining constitutes a cultural tradition deeply ingrained in Istanbul's societal fabric, and sellers rely on it for their livelihoods. Eschew disparaging remarks or disrespectful gestures, as such conduct disrupts harmony and undermines the bargaining dynamic.

By adhering to these guidelines, you'll navigate the intricacies of bargaining with poise and efficacy, securing optimal value for your purchases while honoring Turkish customs and traditions. Embrace the exhilaration of striking a favorable deal at Istanbul's markets and souvenir shops, leveraging your negotiation skills to unlock unparalleled savings and cultural insights.

Free Or Low-Cost Cultural Experiences

Discovering Istanbul's cultural treasures doesn't have to come with a hefty price tag. This vibrant city is teeming with free or low-cost cultural experiences that provide visitors with ample opportunities to immerse themselves in its history, art, and heritage without breaking the bank. From ancient landmarks to contemporary art galleries, Istanbul offers something for everyone to enjoy. In this guide, we'll delve into some of the best free or low-cost cultural experiences for visitors, helping you maximize your time in this dynamic city without straining your wallet.

Exploring Sultanahmet District:
At the heart of historic Istanbul lies the Sultanahmet district, home to some of the city's most iconic landmarks and attractions. Many of these sites are either free to visit or accessible at a nominal cost, making them ideal for budget-conscious travelers.

Begin your exploration at Sultanahmet Square, where you'll encounter the magnificent Blue Mosque, one of Istanbul's most renowned landmarks. While entrance to the mosque is free, contributions towards its maintenance are appreciated. Take your time to marvel at the mosque's breathtaking architecture and tranquil ambiance as you wander through its expansive courtyard and intricate interiors.

From there, make your way to the Hagia Sophia, a UNESCO World Heritage Site with a rich history spanning over a millennium. While there is an admission fee to access the museum, it's a worthwhile investment to behold its majestic dome, intricate mosaics, and layers of historical significance.

After your visit to the Hagia Sophia, take a leisurely stroll through the Hippodrome of Constantinople, an ancient chariot racing track that once stood at the center of Byzantine life. Today, the Hippodrome serves as a public park adorned with ancient monuments and statues, offering visitors a glimpse into Istanbul's storied past.

Exploring the Grand Bazaar:
No trip to Istanbul is complete without a visit to the Grand Bazaar, one of the world's oldest and largest covered markets. While shopping at the Grand Bazaar can be a sensory overload, you don't need to splurge to soak in its vibrant atmosphere and cultural heritage.

Embark on a leisurely wander through the bazaar's maze-like alleys and bustling courtyards, immersing yourself in the sights, sounds, and aromas of this historic marketplace. Admire the intricate architecture, vibrant displays, and diverse array of goods on offer, from handmade carpets and ceramics to aromatic spices and unique souvenirs.

While it may be tempting to indulge in shopping, remember that bargaining is a time-honored tradition at the Grand Bazaar. Put your negotiation skills to the test as you engage with vendors to secure the best possible prices, or simply relish the experience of browsing and window-shopping without making a purchase.

Visiting Istanbul Modern:
For art enthusiasts seeking budget-friendly experiences, a trip to the Istanbul Modern is a must. Situated along the shores of the Bosphorus, this contemporary art museum showcases a diverse collection of Turkish and international art, spanning painting, sculpture, photography, and video installations.

While there is an admission fee for museum entry, it remains relatively affordable compared to similar institutions worldwide, making it accessible to budget-conscious visitors. Moreover, the museum offers free admission on Thursdays, providing an opportune moment to explore its galleries and exhibitions without spending a penny.

In addition to its permanent collection, Istanbul Modern hosts a range of events, workshops, and screenings, many of which are either free or available at a nominal cost. Consult the museum's schedule of events on its website to plan your visit accordingly and take advantage of these enriching cultural offerings.

Taking a Ferry Ride on the Bosphorus:

To experience Istanbul's stunning skyline and picturesque waterfront, consider embarking on a ferry ride along the Bosphorus. While there is a modest fee for ferry tickets, it represents a budget-friendly means of enjoying panoramic views of the city's historic landmarks and natural splendor.

Board a public ferry at Eminonu or Karakoy and cruise along the Bosphorus, passing by iconic sights such as the Maiden's Tower, Dolmabahce Palace, and Ortakoy Mosque. Opt for a clear, sunny day to maximize visibility and relish the unparalleled vistas of the city.

For an even more economical option, consider riding a commuter ferry instead of a tourist cruise. Commuter ferries are both cheaper and provide a more authentic experience, allowing you to mingle with locals and gain insight into everyday life as you traverse the Bosphorus.

Exploring Neighborhoods Off the Beaten Path:
While Sultanahmet and Taksim may be the most frequented tourist hubs in Istanbul, several lesser-known neighborhoods offer distinctive cultural experiences at a fraction of the cost.

Venture to Kadikoy on the Asian side of Istanbul to explore its vibrant markets, quaint cafes, and bustling waterfront promenade. Amble through the Kadikoy Market to sample fresh produce, local delicacies, and street food delights, or peruse the boutiques and shops along Bagdat Avenue for unique souvenirs.

Another hidden gem worth discovering is the Balat neighborhood, renowned for its colorful houses, cobblestone streets, and multicultural ambiance. Take a leisurely stroll through Balat's narrow alleyways and uncover hidden treasures such as the Church of St. Stephen and the Greek Orthodox Patriarchate.

For a taste of Istanbul's bohemian flair, venture to the Beyoglu district and explore its eclectic streets, trendy cafes, and art galleries. Visit the Istanbul Modern, meander down Istiklal Avenue, and bask in the lively ambiance of this dynamic neighborhood.

Attending Cultural Events and Festivals:
Throughout the year, Istanbul hosts a myriad of cultural events and festivals celebrating its rich heritage and diverse communities. Many of these events are either free or available at a nominal cost, offering visitors an opportunity to immerse themselves in Turkish culture firsthand.

Among the city's most anticipated events is the Istanbul Biennial, a biennial contemporary art exhibition held at various venues across Istanbul. Showcasing works by both Turkish and international artists, the biennial serves as a platform for exploring cutting-edge art and addressing pertinent issues.

For aficionados of music, the Istanbul Jazz Festival is a highlight, featuring performances by jazz musicians from around the globe in venues throughout the city. From intimate club concerts to outdoor performances in historic squares, the festival caters to a diverse audience.

Other notable cultural events and festivals in Istanbul include the Istanbul Film Festival, the Istanbul Design Biennial, and the Istanbul International Literature Festival. Consult the city's event calendar to stay abreast of upcoming cultural happenings and plan your visit accordingly to partake in these enriching experiences.

Participating in Free Walking Tours:
Embarking on a free walking tour is an excellent means of acquainting oneself with Istanbul's neighborhoods and landmarks. Led by knowledgeable local guides, these tours provide an insider's perspective on the city's history, culture,

and architecture, enabling you to uncover hidden gems and lesser-known attractions.

Several tour companies in Istanbul offer complimentary walking tours covering a range of themes and locales. Whether you're interested in exploring Sultanahmet's historical sites or delving into the culinary delights of Beyoglu, there's a tour tailored to every interest and budget.

While the tours themselves are free, it's customary to tip your guide at the conclusion of the tour as a token of appreciation for their time and expertise. Remember to factor this into your budget and carry cash with you to tip your guide accordingly.

Exploring Free Museums and Galleries:
In addition to the Istanbul Modern, several other museums and galleries in Istanbul extend free admission to visitors on designated days or times. Capitalize on these opportunities to delve into the city's cultural heritage and artistic offerings without incurring additional expenses.

From the Museum of Turkish and Islamic Arts to the Istanbul Archaeological Museums, there's no shortage of institutions offering complimentary entry to patrons. Consult the websites of individual museums and galleries for information on free admission days and plan your itinerary accordingly to maximize your cultural exploration.

Istanbul's cultural riches are accessible to all, regardless of budget constraints. By taking advantage of free or low-cost cultural experiences, visitors can immerse themselves in the city's history, art, and heritage without overspending. Whether you're exploring historic landmarks, perusing bustling markets, or attending cultural events, Istanbul offers an abundance of opportunities for enriching experiences that won't break the bank. So pack your bags, embark on an adventure, and discover the myriad cultural delights that await you in this captivating city.

Chapter 5

MOVING AROUND AND SLEEPING OVER

Navigating Istanbul's Public Tranportation System

Istanbul, the vibrant and sprawling metropolis straddling two continents, offers a complex but efficient public transportation network that makes getting around the city a breeze for visitors and locals alike. From ferries crisscrossing the Bosphorus to modern trams traversing historic neighborhoods, Istanbul's public transportation system provides convenient and affordable options for exploring the city's rich cultural heritage and diverse attractions. In this comprehensive guide, we'll delve into the various modes of public transportation available in Istanbul, offering tips and insights to help you navigate the city with ease and confidence.

1. Understanding the System:
Before embarking on your journey through Istanbul, it's essential to familiarize yourself with the city's public transportation system. Istanbul's network includes a diverse range of modes, including buses, trams, metro, ferries, and funiculars, all operated by

different authorities but integrated into a unified system.

The Istanbul Metropolitan Municipality (İETT) operates the majority of the city's buses, trams, and ferries, while the Istanbul Metro provides rapid transit services via metro and funicular lines. Additionally, private ferry companies offer services across the Bosphorus and to nearby islands, providing an alternative mode of transportation.

Navigating the system may seem daunting at first, but with a bit of preparation and knowledge, you'll soon discover that getting around Istanbul is easier than you think.

2. Istanbulkart: Your Ticket to Ride:
The Istanbulkart is the city's unified electronic fare payment system, allowing passengers to travel seamlessly across various modes of transportation using a single card. Available for purchase at designated vending machines and kiosks throughout the city, the Istanbulkart offers discounted fares compared to single tickets and provides added convenience for frequent travelers.

To use the Istanbulkart, simply load credit onto the card and tap it on the card reader when boarding a bus, tram, metro, or ferry. The fare will be automatically deducted from your balance, eliminating the need for exact change or paper tickets. Additionally, the Istanbulkart offers transfer privileges within a certain time frame, allowing you to switch between different modes of transportation without paying an additional fare.

3. Metro and Tram:
The Istanbul Metro and tram systems provide rapid transit services connecting key neighborhoods and attractions across the city. The metro network consists of several lines that crisscross Istanbul, providing fast and efficient transportation between distant locations.

The M1 line, for example, connects Ataturk Airport to the city center, while the M2 line traverses the European side of the city from north to south, passing through major hubs such as Taksim Square and Levent. The tram network, on the other hand, serves more localized routes within the city center, providing convenient access to popular tourist destinations such as Sultanahmet and Eminonu.

Both the metro and tram systems operate from early morning until late at night, with trains running at frequent intervals throughout the day. Consult the Istanbul Metro map for route information and timetables, and plan your journey accordingly to avoid long wait times.

4. Bus:
Istanbul's extensive bus network offers comprehensive coverage of the city, making it a convenient and affordable option for getting around. With over a thousand routes serving every corner of Istanbul, buses provide a flexible and accessible mode of transportation for passengers of all ages and abilities.

The Istanbul Metropolitan Municipality operates the majority of the city's buses, with different routes serving specific neighborhoods, districts, and attractions. From modern air-conditioned coaches to traditional dolmus minibusses, there's a bus service to suit every traveler's needs and preferences.

When using the bus system, it's essential to be mindful of peak hours and traffic congestion, which can significantly impact travel times. Plan your journey accordingly, and consider using alternative modes of transportation during busy periods to avoid delays.

5. Ferry:
As a city situated on the banks of the Bosphorus, ferries play a crucial role in Istanbul's public

transportation network, providing essential links between the European and Asian sides of the city. Operated by both public and private companies, ferries offer a scenic and efficient way to travel across the Bosphorus and explore Istanbul's waterfront neighborhoods and landmarks.

Several ferry routes operate between key hubs such as Eminonu, Karakoy, Besiktas, and Uskudar, with frequent departures throughout the day. Whether you're commuting to work, visiting a friend, or simply enjoying a leisurely cruise along the Bosphorus, ferries provide an unforgettable experience that captures the essence of Istanbul's maritime heritage.

6. Funicular:
For travelers navigating Istanbul's hilly terrain, funiculars offer a convenient and time-saving alternative to climbing steep streets and staircases. These inclined railways operate on short routes connecting lower and upper levels of the city, providing easy access to popular destinations such as Taksim Square and the Galata Tower.

The Taksim-Kabatas Funicular, for example, connects Taksim Square with the Kabatas waterfront, where passengers can transfer to ferries and other modes of transportation. Similarly, the

Karakoy-Tunel Funicular provides a quick and efficient link between the Karakoy waterfront and the historic Tunel district, home to Istanbul's oldest underground railway.

7. Tips for Navigating: Navigating Istanbul's public transportation system can be a breeze with a few helpful tips and strategies. Here are some pointers to keep in mind:

- Plan your journey in advance using online resources such as the Istanbul Metro website and mobile apps. Check for route maps, timetables, and service updates to ensure a smooth and hassle-free commute.

- Be prepared for crowded conditions, especially during peak hours and tourist seasons. Consider traveling outside of rush hours to avoid overcrowded vehicles and long wait times.

- Keep your Istanbulkart topped up with sufficient credit to cover your travel expenses. You can reload your card at designated vending machines, kiosks, and authorized retailers throughout the city.

- Be vigilant and aware of your surroundings when using public transportation, especially in crowded areas and tourist hotspots. Keep your belongings secure and beware of pickpockets and scams.

- Take advantage of transfer privileges offered by the Istanbulkart to switch between different modes of transportation without paying an additional fare. This can save you time and money when navigating the city.

By following these tips and utilizing the resources available, you can navigate Istanbul's public transportation system with confidence and ease, allowing you to explore the city's diverse neighborhoods, landmarks, and attractions with ease and efficiency. Whether you're commuting to work, sightseeing, or simply enjoying a leisurely cruise along the Bosphorus, Istanbul's public transportation system offers a convenient and affordable way to get around the city and make the most of your time in this vibrant and dynamic metropolis.

Choosing The Right Accommodations: Hotels, hostels And More

Embarking on a memorable journey through Istanbul begins with selecting the ideal place to stay. Nestled between two continents, Istanbul boasts a diverse array of accommodations catering to every budget, preference, and travel style. From opulent hotels with Bosphorus views to quaint guesthouses nestled in historic quarters, there's a lodging option tailored to suit every traveler's needs. In this comprehensive guide, we'll delve into the various accommodation types available in Istanbul and offer insights to assist you in selecting the perfect option for your requirements and desires.

1. Understanding Your Options: Before diving into accommodation selection, it's crucial to acquaint yourself with the diverse range of lodging options available in Istanbul, each offering unique amenities, features, and price points. Here's a glimpse at some of the most prevalent accommodation types you'll encounter in Istanbul:

- Hotels: Istanbul boasts a plethora of hotels, ranging from luxurious five-star establishments to charming boutique properties. These accommodations offer an array of amenities, including on-site dining, concierge services, and recreational facilities, ensuring a seamless and comfortable stay for guests seeking full-service accommodations.

- Hostels: Catering to budget-conscious travelers and backpackers, hostels provide economical lodging options in shared dormitories or private rooms. While lacking some of the luxuries found in hotels, hostels often foster a social atmosphere with communal spaces and organized activities, making them popular among solo adventurers and young travelers.

- Guesthouses and Bed & Breakfasts: For those craving a more intimate and personalized experience, guesthouses and bed & breakfasts offer cozy accommodations in residential neighborhoods and historic enclaves. These family-run establishments often provide homemade breakfasts, insider tips, and a welcoming ambiance, fostering a sense of home away from home.

- Vacation Rentals: With the advent of platforms like Airbnb and Vrbo, vacation rentals have surged in popularity, offering travelers flexibility, privacy, and authenticity. Ranging from chic apartments in trendy districts to traditional dwellings in historic locales, vacation rentals cater to diverse tastes and budgets, providing a local-centric lodging experience.

- Boutique and Design Hotels: Infusing style, sophistication, and personalized service, boutique and design hotels offer a distinct and memorable stay for discerning travelers. These intimate properties prioritize stylish decor, innovative amenities, and a focus on local culture and design, appealing to those seeking an immersive and upscale experience.

2. Factors to Consider: When selecting accommodations in Istanbul, several factors warrant consideration to ensure a pleasurable and fulfilling stay. Here are key aspects to ponder when evaluating lodging options:

- Location: The locale of your accommodations significantly influences your Istanbul experience. Factor in considerations such as proximity to attractions, public transportation accessibility, dining options, and safety when deciding on a lodging locale. Opting for centrally situated accommodations facilitates efficient exploration and enhances convenience during your stay.

- Amenities and Services: Assess the amenities and services offered by prospective accommodations, such as dining options, fitness facilities, Wi-Fi access, and concierge assistance. Identify amenities crucial for your comfort and convenience, prioritizing lodgings that align with your needs and preferences.

- Reviews and Ratings: Prior to booking, peruse reviews and ratings from previous guests to gauge the quality, cleanliness, and service standards of potential accommodations. Platforms like TripAdvisor, Booking.com, and Google Reviews furnish valuable insights and firsthand feedback, aiding in informed decision-making.

- Price and Value: Establish a budget for lodging expenditures and compare prices and value propositions across various properties. While cost is a significant factor, prioritize value over the cheapest option, considering factors like location, amenities, and guest feedback to ascertain overall value.

- Accessibility: Communicate any specific accessibility requirements or preferences—such as wheelchair accessibility, elevator availability, or dietary constraints—to prospective accommodations in advance to ensure a seamless and accommodating stay.

3. Tips for Booking: After narrowing down your lodging options, follow these tips to streamline the booking process and secure a delightful stay:

- Book in Advance: To secure favorable rates and availability, contemplate booking accommodations well in advance, particularly during peak travel seasons and holidays. Advance planning mitigates last-minute stress and guarantees a comfortable haven during your Istanbul sojourn.

- Flexible Booking Policies: Favor accommodations offering flexible booking policies, encompassing features like free cancellation or modifications, to accommodate unexpected changes in your travel plans. Flexible policies afford added peace of mind and flexibility, empowering you to adjust your itinerary sans penalties.

- Special Offers and Discounts: Stay vigilant for special offers, discounts, and promotions proffered by hotels, hostels, and other lodging establishments in Istanbul. Subscribe to newsletters, monitor social media channels, and enroll in loyalty programs to capitalize on exclusive deals and savings opportunities.

- Direct Communication: For queries or requests pertaining to accommodations—be it dietary specifications, room preferences, or assistance requisites—reach out to properties directly to address your needs. Direct communication fosters a personalized and tailored lodging experience, ensuring optimal comfort and satisfaction.

- Packing Essentials: Before embarking on your journey, assemble essential items like travel adapters, toiletries, medications, and pertinent documentation. Consider carrying a printed copy of your reservation confirmation and lodging contact information to navigate unforeseen circumstances or emergencies seamlessly.

Selecting the perfect accommodations is paramount to orchestrating a fulfilling and enjoyable sojourn in Istanbul. By acquainting yourself with lodging options, weighing key considerations, and adhering to booking tips, you can secure a lodging sanctuary that caters to your needs, preferences, and budget. Whether you covet the indulgence of a luxury hotel, the camaraderie of a hostel, or the intimacy of a boutique guesthouse, Istanbul presents a myriad of accommodations tailored to diverse traveler styles and tastes. So pack your bags, finalize your reservations, and prepare to embark on an unforgettable exploration of Istanbul's charms in comfort and style.

HOTELS

Exploring Istanbul's myriad charms begins with finding the perfect place to stay. Fortunately, this vibrant city offers an array of hotels catering to every taste and budget. Whether you seek luxury, convenience, or cultural immersion, Istanbul has something to offer. Here's a curated selection of hotels in Istanbul that are sure to enhance your visit:

1. Four Seasons Hotel Istanbul at Sultanahmet:

- Located in the heart of historic Sultanahmet, this five-star hotel offers unparalleled luxury and elegance.

- Enjoy stunning views of the Hagia Sophia and Blue Mosque from your room or suite.

- Immerse yourself in Ottoman-inspired architecture and design, complemented by world-class amenities and service.

2. Pera Palace Hotel:

- A historic landmark dating back to 1892, Pera Palace Hotel exudes old-world charm and sophistication.

- Situated in the lively Beyoglu district, this luxury hotel has hosted luminaries such as Agatha Christie and Ernest Hemingway.

- Indulge in opulent accommodations, gourmet dining, and pampering spa treatments at this iconic Istanbul institution.

3. Rixos Pera Istanbul:

- Nestled in the heart of Beyoglu, Rixos Pera Istanbul offers contemporary luxury and panoramic city views.

- Unwind in stylish rooms and suites featuring modern amenities and elegant decor.

- Explore nearby attractions such as Istiklal Avenue, Taksim Square, and the Galata Tower, all within walking distance of the hotel.

4. W Istanbul:
- Embrace Istanbul's vibrant energy at W Istanbul, located in the trendy Akaretler neighborhood.
- Experience modern luxury in rooms and suites adorned with bold design elements and upscale amenities.
- Indulge in innovative cuisine at the hotel's restaurants, or unwind with cocktails at the stylish W Lounge.

5. CVK Park Bosphorus Hotel Istanbul:
- Situated on the shores of the Bosphorus, CVK Park Bosphorus Hotel offers breathtaking views and refined luxury.
- Relax in spacious rooms and suites featuring contemporary decor and state-of-the-art technology.
- Pamper yourself at the hotel's spa, swim in the indoor pool, or savor gourmet cuisine at one of its restaurants.

6. Swissotel The Bosphorus Istanbul:
- Enjoy unparalleled views of the Bosphorus Strait and Istanbul skyline from this five-star hotel.
- Relax in luxurious rooms and suites with modern amenities and elegant decor.

- Take advantage of the hotel's extensive leisure facilities, including a spa, fitness center, and outdoor pool overlooking the Bosphorus.

7. Soho House Istanbul:
- Located in a restored 19th-century building in the trendy Beyoglu district, Soho House Istanbul offers a chic and stylish retreat.
- Stay in beautifully appointed rooms and suites featuring contemporary design and vintage-inspired furnishings.
- Enjoy exclusive amenities such as a rooftop pool, screening room, and members-only club spaces.

8. Georges Hotel Galata:
- Nestled in the historic Galata neighborhood, Georges Hotel Galata offers boutique luxury with panoramic views of the Golden Horn.
- Stay in stylish rooms and suites adorned with contemporary artwork and designer furnishings.
- Relax on the hotel's rooftop terrace, savoring cocktails and Mediterranean cuisine while taking in the stunning Istanbul skyline.

Whether you're seeking historic grandeur, contemporary chic, or panoramic views, these hotels in Istanbul promise an unforgettable experience for every visitor. Book your stay and prepare to immerse yourself in the magic of this enchanting city.

HOSTELS

For budget-conscious travelers and those seeking a vibrant social atmosphere, hostels in Istanbul offer comfortable accommodations and opportunities to connect with fellow visitors from around the world. Here are some top hostels in Istanbul for visitors to consider:

1. Istanbul Hostel
   - Located in the heart of Sultanahmet, Istanbul Hostel offers easy access to major attractions such as the Hagia Sophia and Blue Mosque.
   - Choose from dormitory-style rooms or private rooms with ensuite bathrooms.
   - Enjoy complimentary breakfast, free Wi-Fi, and a cozy common area where you can socialize with other guests.

2. Cheers Hostel
   - Situated near Taksim Square in the lively Beyoglu district, Cheers Hostel is surrounded by restaurants, bars, and nightlife options.
   - Stay in dormitory-style rooms or private rooms with shared bathrooms.

- Take advantage of the hostel's rooftop terrace, where you can enjoy panoramic views of the city while sipping on a drink from the onsite bar.

3. Bunk Hostel

- Located in the historic Sultanahmet district, Bunk Hostel offers affordable accommodations within walking distance of major attractions.
- Choose from mixed or female-only dormitories, as well as private rooms with ensuite bathrooms.
- Relax in the hostel's courtyard garden or socialize with other guests in the communal lounge area.

4. Hush Hostel Lounge

- Situated in the trendy Kadikoy neighborhood on the Asian side of Istanbul, Hush Hostel Lounge offers a laid-back atmosphere and easy access to local markets and waterfront promenades.
- Stay in dormitory-style rooms or private rooms with shared bathrooms.
- Enjoy complimentary breakfast, free Wi-Fi, and nightly events such as movie nights and pub crawls.

5. Bahaus Hostel

- Located in the heart of Beyoglu, Bahaus Hostel is a short walk from Istiklal Avenue, Galata Tower, and other attractions.

- Choose from mixed or female-only dormitories, as well as private rooms with ensuite bathrooms.

- Relax in the hostel's common area, equipped with a TV, board games, and a library, or join one of the hostel's organized walking tours or cooking classes.

6. Bada Bing Hostel

- Situated in the lively Beyoglu district, Bada Bing Hostel offers budget-friendly accommodations close to popular nightlife spots and cultural attractions.

- Stay in dormitory-style rooms or private rooms with shared bathrooms.

- Take advantage of the hostel's communal kitchen, rooftop terrace, and 24-hour reception desk.

7. Hush Hostel Moda

- Located in the Kadikoy district on the Asian side of Istanbul, Hush Hostel Moda offers a relaxed atmosphere and easy access to local cafes, restaurants, and markets.

- Choose from mixed or female-only dormitories, as well as private rooms with shared bathrooms.

- Enjoy complimentary breakfast, free Wi-Fi, and a communal lounge area where you can socialize with other guests.

These hostels in Istanbul provide affordable accommodations, friendly atmospheres, and convenient locations for visitors looking to explore the city on a budget. Whether you're traveling solo, with friends, or as a couple, these hostels offer a welcoming environment and opportunities to connect with fellow travelers from around the world.

Tips For Booking Affordable And Convenient Accommodations

Finding affordable and convenient accommodations is essential for travelers looking to make the most of their visit to Istanbul without breaking the bank. With a wide range of options available, from budget-friendly hostels to boutique hotels, there are plenty of opportunities to find accommodations that meet your needs and budget. In this guide, we'll explore some tips and strategies for booking affordable and convenient accommodations in Istanbul, helping you save money while enjoying a comfortable and memorable stay in this vibrant city.

1. Plan Ahead:
One of the most effective ways to find affordable accommodations in Istanbul is to plan your trip well in advance. By booking your accommodations early, you'll have access to a wider range of options

and can take advantage of lower prices before they rise closer to your travel dates. Additionally, booking in advance allows you to secure your preferred room type and location, ensuring a more convenient and stress-free stay.

2. Be Flexible with Your Travel Dates:
Flexibility is key when it comes to finding affordable accommodations in Istanbul. Consider traveling during off-peak seasons or mid-week, when prices are typically lower and availability is higher. Avoiding major holidays and events can also help you save money on accommodations, as demand is often higher during these times. By being flexible with your travel dates, you can take advantage of lower prices and find better deals on accommodations in Istanbul.

3. Compare Prices and Reviews:
Before booking accommodations in Istanbul, take the time to compare prices and read reviews from previous guests. Websites and platforms such as Booking.com, TripAdvisor, and Airbnb allow you to compare prices, amenities, and guest reviews for different properties, helping you make an informed decision. Pay attention to factors such as location, cleanliness, and customer service when reading reviews, as these can greatly impact your overall experience.

4. Consider Alternative Accommodations:
In addition to traditional hotels and hostels, consider alternative accommodations such as guesthouses, bed & breakfasts, and vacation rentals. These options often offer more affordable rates and a unique, personalized experience that can enhance your stay in Istanbul. Look for properties with positive reviews and reputable hosts to ensure a comfortable and enjoyable stay.

5. Take Advantage of Discounts and Promotions:
Many accommodations in Istanbul offer discounts and promotions to attract guests and fill empty rooms. Keep an eye out for special offers, deals, and last-minute discounts when booking accommodations, as these can help you save money on your stay. Subscribe to newsletters, follow social media accounts, and join loyalty programs to stay informed about exclusive discounts and savings opportunities.

6. Book Directly with the Property:
While third-party booking websites can be convenient for comparing prices and finding deals, consider booking directly with the property whenever possible. Booking directly often allows you to access exclusive discounts and promotions not available through third-party websites, saving

you money on your accommodations. Additionally, booking directly with the property provides a direct line of communication with the staff, allowing you to make special requests or inquire about additional amenities.

7. Look for Hidden Fees:
Before booking accommodations in Istanbul, be sure to read the fine print and look for any hidden fees or additional charges. Some properties may charge extra for amenities such as Wi-Fi, breakfast, parking, or resort fees, which can significantly increase the overall cost of your stay. Factor these fees into your budget when comparing prices and booking accommodations to avoid any surprises upon check-in.

8. Consider Location and Transportation:
When booking accommodations in Istanbul, consider the location and proximity to public transportation, attractions, and amenities. Opting for accommodations in centrally located neighborhoods or near public transportation hubs can save you time and money on transportation costs during your stay. Additionally, staying within walking distance of major attractions and points of interest can help you maximize your time and make the most of your visit to Istanbul.

9. Use Reward Points and Travel Rewards:

If you're a member of a hotel loyalty program or travel rewards program, consider using your reward points or miles to book accommodations in Istanbul. Many hotels and travel companies offer rewards programs that allow you to earn points or miles for every dollar spent on accommodations, which can be redeemed for free nights or discounts on future stays. Take advantage of these rewards programs to save money on your accommodations and make the most of your travel budget.

10. Be Prepared to Negotiate:

Finally, don't be afraid to negotiate with the property directly when booking accommodations in Istanbul. While not all properties may be willing to negotiate on price, some may offer discounts or additional perks if you ask. Be polite, respectful, and flexible when negotiating, and be prepared to walk away if the property is unwilling to meet your terms. With a bit of patience and persistence, you may be able to secure a better deal on your accommodations and save money on your stay in Istanbul.

Booking affordable and convenient accommodations in Istanbul is possible with the right strategies and tips. By planning ahead, being flexible with your travel dates, comparing prices and reviews, and taking advantage of discounts and promotions, you can find accommodations that meet your needs and budget while enjoying a comfortable and memorable stay in this vibrant city. Whether you prefer the luxury of a five-star hotel, the affordability of a hostel, or the charm of a guesthouse, Istanbul offers a wide range of options to suit every traveler's style and preferences. So start planning your trip, follow these tips for booking accommodations, and get ready to explore the wonders of Istanbul on a budget.

Chapter 6

EATING AND ADVENTURES

Sampling Turkish Cuisine On A Budget

Istanbul, the cultural capital of Turkey, is renowned for its rich and diverse culinary heritage, offering a tantalizing array of flavors, aromas, and textures that reflect the country's vibrant history and multicultural influences. From savory kebabs and mezes to sweet pastries and desserts, Turkish cuisine is a feast for the senses that captivates visitors from around the world. While dining out in Istanbul can be a luxurious experience, it's also possible to sample the city's delicious fare on a budget, with plenty of affordable options available for budget-conscious travelers. In this guide, we'll explore some tips and strategies for sampling Turkish cuisine on a budget in Istanbul, helping you savor the city's culinary delights without breaking the bank.

1. Explore Local Markets and Street Food:
   One of the best ways to experience Turkish cuisine on a budget is by exploring the city's vibrant markets and sampling street food from local vendors. Istanbul is home to numerous markets, bazaars, and food stalls where you can find a wide variety of affordable and delicious dishes.

Head to the Grand Bazaar or the Spice Bazaar to explore stalls selling a diverse range of snacks, sweets, and street food favorites. Sample classic dishes like simit (sesame-seed bread rings), börek (flaky pastries filled with cheese or meat), and gözleme (thin flatbread stuffed with various fillings) for a quick and satisfying meal on the go.

For a taste of authentic Turkish street food, visit bustling neighborhoods like Eminönü or Kadıköy, where you'll find vendors selling köfte (grilled meatballs), döner kebab (rotating skewers of seasoned meat), and lahmacun (thin crust pizzas topped with minced meat and spices) at affordable prices. Don't forget to wash it all down with a glass of ayran (yogurt drink) or şalgam (fermented turnip juice) for a refreshing and authentic Turkish dining experience.

2. Embrace the Meze Culture:
Meze, small plates of appetizers or snacks served alongside drinks, are an integral part of Turkish cuisine and offer a budget-friendly way to sample a variety of flavors and dishes. Many restaurants and cafes in Istanbul offer meze platters or meze menus that allow you to try a selection of dishes at a reasonable price.

Look for meze restaurants or meyhane (traditional Turkish taverns) in neighborhoods like Beyoğlu or Karaköy, where you can enjoy an array of cold and hot mezes such as hummus, ezme (spicy tomato and pepper dip), sigara börek (fried cheese-filled pastries), and patlıcan salatası (roasted eggplant salad) for a satisfying and affordable meal.

3. Seek Out Local Favorites:
When dining out in Istanbul on a budget, it's essential to seek out local favorites and traditional dishes that offer excellent value for money. Look for restaurants and eateries frequented by locals rather than tourists, as these establishments often offer authentic and affordable fare.

Try classic Turkish dishes like kuru fasulye (white bean stew), mercimek çorbası (lentil soup), and pilav (rice pilaf) at local lokantas (traditional Turkish restaurants) or ocakbaşı (grill houses), where you can enjoy hearty and flavorful meals at modest prices. Don't forget to finish your meal with a cup of Turkish çay (tea) or Türk kahvesi (Turkish coffee) for a true taste of Turkish hospitality.

4. Take Advantage of Set Menus and Lunch Specials:
Many restaurants in Istanbul offer set menus or lunch specials during the day, providing an

affordable and convenient option for budget-conscious diners. Look for restaurants that advertise fixed-price menus or lunch deals, which often include a selection of dishes at a discounted price compared to à la carte options.

Visit restaurants and cafes in popular tourist areas like Sultanahmet or Taksim during lunchtime to take advantage of set menus and lunch specials. Enjoy a satisfying meal of soup, salad, main course, and dessert for a fraction of the cost of a dinner meal, allowing you to sample Turkish cuisine without breaking the bank.

5. Share Dishes and Opt for Vegetarian Options:
Another budget-friendly dining strategy in Istanbul is to share dishes with friends or fellow travelers and opt for vegetarian options, which are often more affordable than meat-based dishes. Many Turkish restaurants offer large portions that can easily be shared among two or more people, allowing you to sample a variety of dishes without overspending.

Look for vegetarian-friendly restaurants or meze bars that offer a wide selection of plant-based dishes such as dolma (stuffed vegetables), pilaki (bean stew), and mücver (zucchini fritters). Sharing several vegetarian dishes with your dining companions allows you to enjoy a diverse and satisfying meal at a reasonable price, making it an ideal option for budget-conscious travelers.

6. Dine Like a Local:

To truly experience Turkish cuisine on a budget, consider dining like a local and embracing the culture of sharing and hospitality that is central to Turkish dining traditions. Instead of dining out at restaurants every night, consider shopping for fresh ingredients at local markets and preparing simple meals at your accommodation.

Visit neighborhood markets like the Kadıköy Fish Market or the Feriköy Organic Market to shop for fresh produce, meats, cheeses, and spices. Then, head back to your accommodation and prepare a traditional Turkish meal such as menemen (scrambled eggs with tomatoes and peppers), karnıyarık (stuffed eggplant), or mantı (Turkish dumplings) in the comfort of your own kitchen.

Not only is cooking your meals a budget-friendly option, but it also allows you to experience the joy of shopping for fresh ingredients, learning new recipes, and sharing meals with friends and fellow travelers. Plus, you'll have the satisfaction of knowing that you're supporting local vendors and producers while reducing your travel expenses.

Sampling Turkish cuisine on a budget in Istanbul is a delicious and rewarding experience that allows you to savor the city's diverse flavors and culinary traditions without breaking the bank. By exploring local markets, sampling street food, embracing the meze culture, seeking out local favorites, taking advantage of set menus and lunch specials, and dining like a local, you can enjoy an authentic and memorable culinary adventure in Istanbul without overspending. So pack your appetite, follow these tips, and get ready to indulge in the delicious tastes of Turkey while staying within your budget.

Hidden Gems: Affordable Local Eateries And Street Food Stalls

Exploring the culinary landscape of Istanbul unveils a vibrant tapestry of flavors, where affordable local eateries and street food stalls shine as hidden gems waiting to be discovered. While high-end restaurants command attention, it's these humble spots that truly capture the essence of Turkish cuisine, offering authentic delights without straining your wallet. Join us on a journey to uncover Istanbul's culinary treasures, where savory kebabs, aromatic mezes, and delectable pastries await at prices that won't break the bank.

1. Embracing Street Food Culture:
In Istanbul, street food isn't just sustenance; it's a way of life. Venture into the bustling streets to encounter a world of culinary delights that cater to every palate and budget.

Simit: Seek out the ubiquitous simit vendors scattered across the city, offering circular bread encrusted with sesame seeds. This quintessential Turkish snack is a pocket-friendly treat enjoyed by locals and visitors alike.

Döner Kebab: Follow the tantalizing aroma to döner kebab stalls, where succulent meat rotates on skewers, ready to be thinly sliced and served in wraps or sandwiches. With options ranging from chicken to lamb, döner kebabs offer a satisfying meal on a budget.

2. Exploring Neighborhood Markets:
Step into the heart of Istanbul's neighborhoods to discover bustling markets teeming with fresh produce, aromatic spices, and local delicacies. These vibrant hubs provide an immersive culinary experience that won't break the bank.

Kadıköy Fish Market: Lose yourself in the sights and sounds of Kadıköy Fish Market, where vendors display an array of seafood delights. Sample freshly shucked oysters, succulent mussels, and other treasures of the sea at affordable prices.

Fatih Çarşamba Market: Navigate the labyrinthine aisles of Fatih Çarşamba Market, where stalls brim with colorful fruits, vegetables, and spices. Don't miss the opportunity to indulge in local specialties like pickles, cured meats, and freshly baked pastries.

3. Sampling Mezes and Snacks:
Embrace the tradition of meze, where small plates of appetizers beckon diners to savor a medley of flavors. Istanbul's local eateries and meyhanes offer an affordable feast of savory delights perfect for sharing with friends.

Beyoğlu and Kadıköy: Wander through the streets of Beyoğlu and Kadıköy to discover hidden gem meyhanes serving up classic meze dishes. From creamy hummus to fiery ezme, these establishments offer an authentic taste of Turkish cuisine at wallet-friendly prices.

Sweet Treats: Indulge your sweet tooth with Istanbul's delectable desserts and pastries, available at bakeries and patisseries throughout the city. Sink your teeth into baklava, a heavenly confection of layered filo dough and nuts soaked in syrup, or savor künefe, a warm and gooey delight that's sure to satisfy.

4. Seeking Local Favorites:
For an authentic dining experience that won't break the bank, follow the locals to their favorite haunts. From family-run kebab shops to hole-in-the-wall cafes, these hidden gems promise culinary delights that won't disappoint.

Ask the Locals: Tap into the insider knowledge of locals or scour online resources to uncover Istanbul's best-kept secrets. Look for bustling eateries with long lines or crowded tables, a sure sign of quality and popularity among locals.

Affordable Dining Tips: Dining on a budget in Istanbul is easier than you think. Set a budget, share meals with friends, and take advantage of lunch specials and BYOB policies to make the most of your culinary adventures without overspending.

Exploring Istanbul's affordable local eateries and street food stalls is a journey of culinary discovery that promises an authentic and unforgettable experience. From the savory delights of street-side kebabs to the sweet indulgence of Turkish pastries, these hidden gems offer a taste of Istanbul's rich culinary heritage at prices that won't break the bank.

So pack your appetite, follow our guide, and embark on a culinary adventure through the streets of Istanbul to uncover affordable and delicious eats that will leave you craving more.

Outdoor Adventures: Hiking, Biking And Beyond

While Istanbul is famous for its rich history, vibrant culture, and delicious cuisine, it also boasts a diverse array of outdoor adventures for nature lovers and outdoor enthusiasts. From scenic hikes and exhilarating bike rides to thrilling water sports and tranquil parks, Istanbul offers endless opportunities for outdoor exploration and adventure. In this guide, we'll delve into the outdoor adventures awaiting travelers in Istanbul, from the iconic trails of the Bosphorus to the hidden gems of the Princes' Islands, inviting you to discover the city's natural beauty and outdoor wonders.

1. Hiking Trails: Despite being a bustling metropolis, Istanbul is home to numerous hiking trails and scenic paths that offer a welcome escape from the city's urban hustle and bustle. From coastal promenades to forested hillsides, these trails provide an opportunity to immerse yourself in nature and enjoy breathtaking views of the city and surrounding landscapes.

a. Belgrade Forest:

Located on the outskirts of Istanbul, the Belgrade Forest offers a tranquil retreat from the city's chaos, with miles of hiking trails winding through lush greenery and towering trees. Follow the paths that crisscross the forest, passing by serene ponds, meandering streams, and centuries-old trees as you explore this natural oasis. The Belgrade Forest is also home to the Atatürk Arboretum, a botanical garden showcasing a diverse collection of plant species from around the world, making it a must-visit destination for nature lovers and botany enthusiasts alike.

b. Camlica Hill:

For panoramic views of Istanbul's skyline and the shimmering waters of the Bosphorus, head to Camlica Hill, one of the highest points in the city. A network of hiking trails leads to the summit of the hill, where you'll be rewarded with sweeping vistas of the city below. Whether you choose to hike to the top or take a leisurely stroll along the scenic paths, a visit to Camlica Hill promises breathtaking views and unforgettable memories.

c. Princes' Islands:

Just a short ferry ride from the city center, the Princes' Islands offer a peaceful retreat from the hustle and bustle of Istanbul, with car-free streets, lush green landscapes, and picturesque hiking trails waiting to be explored. Rent a bike or lace up your hiking boots and embark on a journey to discover the island's hidden gems, from secluded beaches and historic churches to scenic viewpoints and charming villages. With its tranquil atmosphere and stunning natural beauty, the Princes' Islands are the perfect destination for a day of outdoor adventure and exploration.

2. Biking Routes: With its flat terrain, scenic waterfronts, and well-maintained bike paths, Istanbul is a paradise for cyclists of all skill levels. Whether you're a seasoned cyclist or a casual rider, there are plenty of biking routes to explore in and around the city, offering a fun and eco-friendly way to see the sights and soak up the scenery.

a. Bosphorus Bike Path:

Stretching along the shores of the Bosphorus, the Bosphorus Bike Path offers a scenic and leisurely route for cyclists to explore Istanbul's iconic waterfront. Starting from the Golden Horn in the north and winding all the way to the Marmara Sea in the south, this picturesque path passes by historic landmarks, lush parks, and charming neighborhoods, providing a unique perspective of the city's beauty and charm. Stop along the way to admire the views, snap photos of the stunning scenery, and refuel with a refreshing drink or snack at one of the many cafes and restaurants lining the route.

b. Princes' Islands:

The car-free streets and scenic landscapes of the Princes' Islands make it an ideal destination for biking enthusiasts looking to explore Istanbul's natural beauty on two wheels. Rent a bike from one of the rental shops on the islands and set off on a leisurely ride along the waterfront promenades, charming villages, and lush green hillsides. With its gentle slopes and picturesque scenery, biking on the Princes' Islands offers a relaxing and enjoyable way to discover the island's hidden gems and escape the hustle and bustle of the city.

c. Atatürk Arboretum:

Located within the Belgrade Forest, the Atatürk Arboretum offers a unique opportunity for cyclists to explore a diverse collection of plant species from around the world while enjoying a scenic bike ride through the forest. Follow the designated bike paths that wind through the arboretum, passing by colorful gardens, tranquil ponds, and shaded groves as you pedal your way through this botanical paradise. With its peaceful atmosphere and natural beauty, the Atatürk Arboretum is a must-visit destination for cyclists looking to escape the city and immerse themselves in nature.

3. Beyond Hiking and Biking: In addition to hiking and biking, Istanbul offers a variety of other outdoor adventures and activities for travelers to enjoy, from water sports and boat tours to picnics in the park and birdwatching excursions.

a. Water Sports:
With its strategic location on the Bosphorus Strait, Istanbul is a playground for water sports enthusiasts, offering a wide range of activities such as kayaking, paddleboarding, and sailing. Head to the shores of the Bosphorus or the Princes' Islands to rent equipment and embark on an aquatic adventure, exploring the city's scenic coastline and hidden coves from a unique perspective.

b. Boat Tours:
For a relaxing and scenic way to see the sights of Istanbul, hop aboard a boat tour and cruise along the Bosphorus, taking in iconic landmarks such as the Maiden's Tower, the Dolmabahçe Palace, and the Rumeli Fortress. Choose from a variety of tour options, including private charters, sunset cruises,

and dinner cruises, and enjoy stunning views of the city's skyline and waterfront as you glide along the shimmering waters of the Bosphorus.

c. Picnics in the Park:
Escape the hustle and bustle of the city and enjoy a peaceful picnic in one of Istanbul's many parks and green spaces. From the sprawling grounds of the Emirgan Park to the scenic shores of the Göksu Park, there are plenty of tranquil spots to spread out a blanket, relax in the shade, and enjoy a leisurely meal al fresco. Pack a basket with local delicacies such as börek, olives, and Turkish delight, and savor the flavors of Istanbul's culinary delights surrounded by nature.

d. Birdwatching Excursions:
For nature lovers and birdwatching enthusiasts, Istanbul offers a variety of opportunities to observe migratory birds and native wildlife in their natural habitat. Head to the wetlands of Lake Küçükçekmece or the forests of the Belgrade Forest to spot a variety of bird species, including herons, flamingos, and kingfishers, as well as mammals such as foxes, deer, and wild boar. Join a guided birdwatching excursion or explore on your own, armed with binoculars and a sense of adventure, and discover the rich biodiversity of Istanbul's natural landscapes.

From scenic hikes and exhilarating bike rides to thrilling water sports and tranquil picnics in the park, Istanbul offers endless opportunities for outdoor adventure and exploration. Whether you're seeking breathtaking views of the city skyline, serene nature trails, or exciting water activities, Istanbul's outdoor adventures promise unforgettable experiences for travelers of all ages and interests. So lace up your hiking boots, grab your bike, and embark on a journey to discover the hidden gems of Istanbul's natural beauty and outdoor wonders, inviting you to explore, discover, and connect with the great outdoors in the heart of the city.

Chapter 7

STAYING SAFE AND GREEN

Safety Tips For Solo Travelers And Tourists

Istanbul, with its rich history, vibrant culture, and bustling streets, is a city that captivates visitors from around the world. However, like any major urban center, Istanbul has its share of safety concerns, and it's essential for solo travelers and tourists to take precautions to ensure a safe and enjoyable experience. In this guide, we'll explore some key safety tips for navigating Istanbul as a solo traveler or tourist, from staying vigilant in crowded areas to avoiding scams and petty crime, empowering you to explore this fascinating city with confidence and peace of mind.

1. Stay Aware of Your Surroundings:
One of the most important safety tips for solo travelers and tourists in Istanbul is to stay aware of your surroundings at all times. Whether you're exploring historic landmarks, shopping in bustling markets, or navigating crowded streets, it's essential to remain vigilant and attentive to your surroundings to avoid potential risks and hazards.

Be mindful of your personal belongings, such as wallets, purses, and smartphones, and keep them secure and out of sight to deter pickpockets and thieves. Avoid displaying expensive jewelry or valuables that may attract unwanted attention and make you a target for theft.

When walking or traveling alone, stick to well-lit and populated areas, especially at night, and trust your instincts if you feel unsafe or uncomfortable in any situation. If you're unsure about a particular neighborhood or area, seek advice from locals or hotel staff before venturing out, and consider using reputable transportation services or ridesharing apps for added security and peace of mind.

2. Dress Appropriately and Respect Local Customs:
  In Istanbul, as in many other cities around the world, it's important to dress appropriately and respect local customs and cultural norms, especially when visiting religious sites, mosques, and conservative neighborhoods. While Istanbul is generally a cosmopolitan and tolerant city, conservative dress is expected in certain areas, particularly in mosques and religious institutions.

When visiting mosques, women should cover their heads with a scarf or shawl and wear modest clothing that covers their shoulders, arms, and legs, while men should wear long pants and avoid wearing shorts or sleeveless shirts. Remove your shoes before entering mosques and other places of worship, and be respectful of religious practices and rituals.

Outside of religious sites, dress modestly and avoid wearing revealing clothing or clothing with offensive slogans or symbols that may offend locals or attract unwanted attention. By dressing respectfully and adhering to local customs, you'll not only show respect for the culture and traditions of Istanbul but also minimize the risk of encountering any negative reactions or confrontations.

3. Use Reliable Transportation Options:
When getting around Istanbul, it's important to use reliable transportation options that prioritize safety and security, especially for solo travelers and tourists. Istanbul has a well-developed public transportation system, including buses, trams, ferries, and the metro, which are generally safe and efficient for getting around the city.

Stick to official taxi stands or use reputable ridesharing apps like Uber or BiTaksi to hail a taxi, and avoid accepting rides from unlicensed or unofficial drivers to minimize the risk of scams or overcharging. Before getting into a taxi, ensure that the meter is running and that the driver is using the most direct route to your destination, and be prepared to negotiate the fare if necessary.

If you prefer to explore Istanbul on foot, stick to well-lit and populated areas, especially at night, and consider using maps or navigation apps to plan your route in advance and avoid getting lost. Be cautious when crossing busy streets or intersections, and always use pedestrian crossings and crosswalks to ensure your safety.

4. Avoid Common Scams and Petty Crime:

Like any major tourist destination, Istanbul has its share of common scams and petty crime, and it's important for solo travelers and tourists to be vigilant and cautious to avoid falling victim to these schemes. Some of the most common scams in Istanbul include:

- The shoe-shine scam: In this scam, a shoe shiner will approach you and offer to shine your shoes for a fee, but then demand an exorbitant amount of money once the job is done. To avoid this scam, politely decline any unsolicited offers for shoe shining services and walk away.

- The overpriced carpet or souvenir scam: In this scam, a friendly local or shopkeeper will invite you into their store or shop and pressure you into purchasing overpriced carpets, rugs, or souvenirs. To avoid this scam, be wary of high-pressure sales tactics and always negotiate the price before making a purchase.

- The fake police officer scam: In this scam, a person posing as a police officer will approach you and ask to see your identification or passport, claiming to be conducting a routine check. To avoid this scam, always ask to see official identification and never hand over your passport or personal belongings to anyone you don't trust.

To protect yourself from common scams and petty crime in Istanbul, it's important to exercise caution and skepticism when interacting with strangers, especially in tourist areas and crowded places. Keep your valuables secure and out of sight, avoid carrying large amounts of cash or displaying expensive electronics, and be wary of anyone who approaches you with unsolicited offers or assistance.

5. Stay Connected and Informed:
Finally, staying connected and informed is essential for solo travelers and tourists in Istanbul,

especially in the event of an emergency or unexpected situation. Make sure to keep your smartphone charged and carry a portable charger or power bank with you to ensure that you can stay in touch with family, friends, or emergency services if needed.

Before traveling to Istanbul, research local emergency contact numbers and information, including the nearest hospitals, police stations, and embassy or consulate offices, and keep this information handy in case of an emergency. Consider downloading useful apps or resources, such as maps, translation tools, and travel guides, to help navigate the city and access important information on the go.

Additionally, stay informed about current events, safety alerts, and travel advisories for Istanbul by checking reputable sources such as government websites, news outlets, and travel advisories issued by your home country. By staying connected and informed, you'll be better prepared to handle any challenges or emergencies that may arise during your travels and enjoy a safe and memorable experience in Istanbul.

Exploring Istanbul as a solo traveler or tourist can be an exciting and rewarding experience, but it's important to prioritize safety and take precautions to ensure a smooth and enjoyable journey. By staying aware of your surroundings, dressing appropriately, using reliable transportation options, avoiding common scams and petty crime, and staying connected and informed, you can navigate Istanbul with confidence and peace of mind, knowing that you're taking steps to protect yourself and enjoy all that this vibrant city has to offer. So pack your bags, follow these safety tips, and get ready for an unforgettable adventure in Istanbul, where every corner is waiting to be explored.

Emergency Contacts And Medical Services

When traveling to a new destination, it's essential to be prepared for any unexpected situations or emergencies that may arise, including accidents, illnesses, or other medical emergencies. Istanbul, like any major city, has a range of emergency services and medical facilities available to assist travelers in times of need. In this guide, we'll explore the emergency contacts and medical services available in Istanbul, helping you stay informed and prepared for any unforeseen circumstances during your visit to this vibrant and dynamic city.

1. Emergency Contact Numbers: In case of an emergency in Istanbul, it's important to know the appropriate contact numbers to call for assistance. The following are some of the essential emergency contact numbers to keep handy:

- Emergency Services (Police, Fire, Ambulance): 112
- Tourist Police: 155
- Coast Guard: 158
- Medical Emergency: 112

These emergency contact numbers can be dialed from any phone, including landlines, mobile phones, and payphones, and are available 24 hours a day, seven days a week, to assist travelers in need of urgent assistance. When calling emergency services, be prepared to provide your location, details of the emergency, and any other relevant information to ensure a prompt and effective response.

2. Medical Facilities and Hospitals: Istanbul is home to a wide range of medical facilities and hospitals that provide high-quality care and treatment for both residents and travelers. Whether you're in need of urgent medical attention or routine healthcare services, there are numerous hospitals,

clinics, and medical centers available throughout the city to address your needs.

Some of the leading hospitals and medical facilities in Istanbul include:

- Acıbadem Healthcare Group: With multiple locations across Istanbul, Acıbadem Healthcare Group is one of the largest and most reputable private healthcare providers in Turkey, offering a wide range of medical services and specialties, including emergency care, surgery, and outpatient services.

- Florence Nightingale Hospital: Located in the Şişli district of Istanbul, Florence Nightingale Hospital is a modern and well-equipped facility offering comprehensive medical care and services, including emergency medicine, surgery, and diagnostic imaging.

- Memorial Şişli Hospital: Situated in the heart of Istanbul, Memorial Şişli Hospital is a leading healthcare institution known for its advanced medical technology, experienced medical staff, and commitment to patient care, offering a full range of medical services and specialties.

- American Hospital Istanbul: Founded in 1920, American Hospital Istanbul is one of the oldest and most respected hospitals in Turkey, providing high-quality healthcare services to patients from around the world, including emergency care, surgery, and specialized treatments.

In addition to these major hospitals, Istanbul also has numerous smaller clinics, medical centers, and pharmacies located throughout the city, offering a range of healthcare services and treatments for minor ailments and injuries. Whether you're in need of emergency medical care or routine healthcare services, you can rest assured that Istanbul has a variety of medical facilities and providers available to meet your needs.

3. Travel Insurance: Before traveling to Istanbul, it's highly recommended to purchase travel insurance that includes coverage for medical emergencies and healthcare services. Travel insurance can provide financial protection and peace of mind in the event of unexpected illnesses, accidents, or injuries while abroad, covering expenses such as hospitalization, medical treatment, emergency medical evacuation, and repatriation of remains.

When purchasing travel insurance, be sure to review the policy details carefully to understand what is covered and excluded, including any pre-existing medical conditions, exclusions, and limitations. Consider choosing a comprehensive travel insurance policy that offers coverage for a wide range of potential emergencies and contingencies, including medical emergencies, trip cancellations, lost baggage, and travel delays.

4. Precautionary Measures: In addition to knowing emergency contact numbers and accessing medical services, there are several precautionary measures that travelers can take to minimize the risk of medical emergencies and stay safe and healthy during their visit to Istanbul:

- Stay hydrated: Drink plenty of water throughout the day, especially in hot weather, to prevent dehydration and heat-related illnesses.

- Practice good hygiene: Wash your hands frequently with soap and water, especially before eating or handling food, to reduce the risk of contracting infectious diseases.

- Protect against sun exposure: Wear sunscreen, sunglasses, and protective clothing to shield yourself from the sun's harmful UV rays and prevent sunburn and heatstroke.

- Carry essential medications: If you take prescription medications regularly, be sure to bring an ample supply with you and carry them in their original packaging to avoid any issues with customs or immigration.

- Be cautious with food and water: Avoid consuming tap water and raw or undercooked foods that may harbor bacteria or parasites, and opt for bottled water and freshly prepared meals from reputable establishments.

By taking these precautionary measures and being prepared with emergency contact numbers and medical services, travelers can enjoy a safe and worry-free experience in Istanbul, knowing that they have access to the necessary resources and support in case of an emergency. With its modern medical facilities, experienced healthcare providers, and commitment to patient care, Istanbul is well-equipped to handle a wide range of medical emergencies and ensure the safety and well-being of travelers from around the world.

Staying safe and healthy while traveling is a top priority for any traveler, and being prepared for emergencies is essential to ensure a smooth and enjoyable experience. By knowing emergency contact numbers, accessing medical services, purchasing travel insurance, and taking precautionary measures, travelers can navigate Istanbul with confidence and peace of mind, knowing that they have the necessary resources and support to address any unexpected situations or emergencies that may arise. Whether you're exploring the city's historic landmarks, shopping in its bustling markets, or enjoying its vibrant culture and cuisine, knowing that you have access to emergency assistance and medical care can provide reassurance and confidence as you explore the sights and sounds of this dynamic and captivating city.

Responsible Tourism: Sustainable Practices In Istanbul

As one of the world's most popular tourist destinations, Istanbul welcomes millions of visitors each year eager to explore its rich history, vibrant culture, and stunning landmarks. However, with the rise in tourism comes the responsibility to ensure that travel and exploration are conducted in a sustainable and responsible manner. Sustainable tourism practices are essential for preserving Istanbul's cultural heritage, protecting its natural environment, and benefiting local communities. In this guide, we'll explore the concept of responsible tourism and highlight sustainable practices that travelers can adopt to minimize their impact on Istanbul's environment and culture while maximizing the benefits to local residents and businesses.

1. Understanding Responsible Tourism:

Responsible tourism is a concept that emphasizes the importance of minimizing negative impacts on the environment, culture, and communities while maximizing the positive benefits of tourism. It encompasses a range of principles and practices aimed at promoting sustainability, ethical behavior, and respect for local customs and traditions. Responsible tourists strive to minimize their ecological footprint, support local businesses and communities, and engage in cultural exchange in a respectful and mindful manner.

In Istanbul, responsible tourism is particularly important due to the city's status as a major cultural and historical hub. By adopting sustainable practices and respecting Istanbul's cultural heritage and natural environment, travelers can contribute to the preservation of the city's unique identity and ensure that future generations can continue to enjoy its beauty and charm.

2. Sustainable Practices for Responsible Tourism in Istanbul:

a. Respect Local Customs and Traditions: One of the most important aspects of responsible tourism is respecting local customs, traditions, and cultural practices. In Istanbul, visitors should familiarize themselves with Turkish customs and etiquette, including appropriate dress codes, greetings, and behaviors in public spaces and religious sites. By showing respect for local customs and traditions, travelers can foster positive interactions with locals and contribute to cultural exchange and understanding.

b. Support Local Businesses and Communities: Supporting local businesses and communities is another key aspect of responsible tourism. Instead of patronizing large chain hotels and international restaurants, travelers should seek out locally owned accommodations, eateries, and shops that contribute to the local economy and employ local residents. By spending money at small businesses and artisans' markets, travelers can directly support local entrepreneurs and artisans and contribute to the economic vitality of Istanbul's neighborhoods and communities.

c. Minimize Environmental Impact: Minimizing environmental impact is essential for promoting sustainable tourism in Istanbul. Travelers can reduce their ecological footprint by conserving water and energy, reducing waste, and minimizing carbon emissions. Simple actions such as using reusable water bottles, opting for public transportation or walking instead of driving, and properly disposing of waste can help reduce the environmental impact of tourism on Istanbul's delicate ecosystems and natural resources.

d. Practice Responsible Wildlife Viewing: When engaging in wildlife viewing activities, such as visiting zoos, aquariums, or wildlife sanctuaries, travelers should choose reputable establishments that prioritize animal welfare and conservation. Avoid supporting facilities that exploit or mistreat animals for entertainment purposes and opt for responsible wildlife experiences that promote education, conservation, and ethical treatment of animals.

e. Leave No Trace: One of the fundamental principles of responsible tourism is leaving no trace and minimizing the impact of tourism activities on natural landscapes and cultural sites. Travelers should avoid littering, vandalism, and other forms of damage to historical monuments, archaeological sites, and natural habitats. Respect posted signage, follow designated trails, and refrain from removing or damaging artifacts or natural resources.

f. Engage in Sustainable Activities: When planning activities and excursions in Istanbul, travelers should prioritize sustainable and eco-friendly options that support conservation efforts and minimize environmental impact. Consider participating in nature walks, birdwatching tours, or eco-friendly boat trips along the Bosphorus to experience Istanbul's natural beauty while supporting conservation initiatives and responsible tourism practices.

By embracing responsible tourism practices, travelers can help protect Istanbul's cultural heritage, preserve its natural environment, and support local communities and economies. From respecting local customs and traditions to minimizing environmental impact and supporting sustainable businesses, responsible tourism offers a pathway to experiencing Istanbul's beauty and charm while leaving a positive legacy for future generations. By incorporating sustainable practices into their travel experiences, travelers can make a meaningful difference and contribute to the long-term sustainability and vitality of Istanbul as a world-class destination for cultural exploration and discovery.

Maps

Reasons For Using Maps:

1. Navigating the City: Istanbul is a vast and sprawling metropolis, spanning two continents and boasting a rich tapestry of neighborhoods, landmarks, and attractions. Navigating its labyrinthine streets and bustling districts can be daunting, especially for first-time visitors. Maps provide an invaluable tool for orienting oneself within the city, helping travelers find their way to key destinations such as historic sites, museums, markets, and restaurants.

2. Discovering Points of Interest: With its wealth of cultural, historical, and architectural attractions, Istanbul offers something for every traveler. However, uncovering hidden gems and lesser-known sites can be challenging without proper guidance. Maps allow tourists to pinpoint points of interest, including off-the-beaten-path neighborhoods, local markets, and scenic viewpoints. By consulting a map, travelers can create personalized itineraries that reflect their interests and preferences, ensuring a memorable and enriching experience.

3. Planning Efficient Routes: Time is precious when exploring a new destination, and travelers often seek to maximize their sightseeing opportunities

while minimizing travel time. Maps enable tourists to plan efficient routes between attractions, optimizing their itinerary to cover the most ground in the shortest amount of time. Whether traveling by foot, public transportation, or taxi, having a map on hand helps visitors navigate the city's transportation network and avoid unnecessary detours or delays.

4. Understanding Public Transport: Istanbul boasts an extensive public transportation system, including buses, trams, ferries, and metro lines, which provide convenient access to various parts of the city. However, navigating the public transport network can be challenging without proper guidance. Maps of Istanbul's public transportation routes help travelers identify the nearest stops, plan their journeys, and navigate transfers between different modes of transport. Additionally, maps often include information on ticket prices, schedules, and service updates, allowing tourists to travel with confidence and ease.

5. Enhancing Safety and Security: In any unfamiliar city, safety is a top priority for travelers. Maps serve as a valuable tool for enhancing safety and security by helping tourists stay aware of their surroundings and avoid potentially hazardous areas. By familiarizing themselves with the layout of the city and identifying well-traveled routes, visitors can

minimize the risk of getting lost or encountering unsafe situations. Furthermore, maps may include information on emergency services, medical facilities, and police stations, providing travelers with essential resources in case of emergencies.

6. Immersing in Local Culture: Beyond practical navigation, maps also offer opportunities for cultural immersion and exploration. Tourists can use maps to identify neighborhoods known for their distinct cultural heritage, such as Sultanahmet with its historic landmarks or Kadıköy with its vibrant arts scene. By venturing off the beaten path and exploring local communities, travelers can gain a deeper appreciation for Istanbul's rich cultural diversity and engage with its residents in meaningful ways.

In summary, maps are indispensable tools for travelers and tourists exploring Istanbul, offering guidance, efficiency, safety, and cultural immersion. By leveraging maps during their visit, tourists can navigate the city with confidence, discover its hidden treasures, and create unforgettable experiences.

Top Maps Apps For Navigating Istanbul

Navigating Istanbul, with its rich history, diverse neighborhoods, and sprawling landscape, can be a delightful yet challenging endeavor for travelers. Fortunately, there are several top maps and navigation tools specifically designed to help visitors explore the city with ease. Here are some of the most popular options:

1. Google Maps: As one of the most widely used mapping services worldwide, Google Maps remains a go-to choice for navigating Istanbul. Its comprehensive coverage of streets, landmarks, and public transportation options makes it invaluable for travelers. With features like real-time traffic updates, walking directions, and street view imagery, Google Maps provides a reliable and user-friendly navigation experience for exploring Istanbul's vibrant streets and neighborhoods.

2. Citymapper: Citymapper is a transit app that offers detailed public transportation information and route planning for cities around the world, including Istanbul. Travelers can use Citymapper to access up-to-date schedules, maps, and directions for buses, trams, ferries, and metro lines in Istanbul. The app also provides real-time arrival information and alerts to help users navigate the city's public transport network efficiently.

3. Moovit: Moovit is another popular app for navigating public transportation in Istanbul. It offers

comprehensive route planning, real-time arrival updates, and service alerts for buses, trams, ferries, and metro lines. Moovit's user-friendly interface and detailed transit maps make it easy for travelers to find the best routes and connections to their desired destinations in Istanbul.

4. Istanbulkart Mobile App: Istanbulkart is the city's official transportation card, used for accessing buses, trams, ferries, and metro lines. The Istanbulkart mobile app allows users to manage their card balance, check transaction history, and top up funds remotely. Additionally, the app provides route planning and real-time arrival information for public transportation services in Istanbul, making it a convenient tool for travelers relying on the city's transit network.

5. Istanbul Offline Map & Guide: For travelers looking for an offline navigation solution, the Istanbul Offline Map & Guide app offers detailed maps, points of interest, and travel tips that can be accessed without an internet connection. The app includes offline navigation features, such as route planning and location search, allowing users to explore Istanbul's streets and attractions without relying on mobile data or Wi-Fi connectivity.

6. Istanbul Official City Guide: The Istanbul Official City Guide app, developed by the Istanbul Metropolitan Municipality, provides tourists with essential information about the city's attractions, events, and services. The app features interactive maps, walking tours, and multimedia guides to help users discover Istanbul's cultural heritage and landmarks. Travelers can use the app to plan their itinerary, find nearby points of interest, and learn about the city's history and culture while exploring its streets.

7. OpenStreetMap: OpenStreetMap (OSM) is a collaborative mapping platform that offers detailed, user-generated maps of cities and regions worldwide, including Istanbul. OSM provides up-to-date street maps, points of interest, and public transportation routes that can be accessed online or downloaded for offline use. Travelers can contribute to OSM by adding or editing map data, ensuring that the information remains accurate and reliable for future visitors to Istanbul.

These top maps and navigation tools offer valuable resources for travelers navigating Istanbul's streets, neighborhoods, and public transportation network. Whether seeking real-time transit information, offline navigation solutions, or comprehensive city guides, these apps and services cater to the diverse needs of visitors exploring the vibrant metropolis of Istanbul.

How To Use Maps Effectively

Using maps effectively is essential for travelers to navigate unfamiliar cities like Istanbul with confidence and ease. Here are some tips to help travelers make the most of their mapping experience:

1. Plan Ahead: Before setting out to explore Istanbul, take some time to familiarize yourself with the city's layout, major landmarks, and points of interest. Use maps to identify key attractions, neighborhoods, and transportation hubs, and plan a rough itinerary to optimize your time and minimize unnecessary travel.

2. Choose the Right Map: Select a reliable mapping service or app that provides accurate and up-to-date information about Istanbul's streets, public transportation routes, and points of interest. Consider factors such as offline functionality, real-time updates, and user-friendly interface when choosing a map for your travels.

3. Download Offline Maps: If you anticipate being in areas with limited or no internet connectivity, download offline maps of Istanbul to your mobile

device beforehand. This will allow you to access maps, directions, and points of interest even when you're offline, ensuring that you can navigate the city without relying on mobile data or Wi-Fi.

4. Customize Your Settings: Adjust the settings of your chosen mapping app to suit your preferences and needs. Enable features like turn-by-turn navigation, real-time traffic updates, and public transportation information to get the most accurate and relevant directions while exploring Istanbul.

5. Use Landmarks as Reference Points: In addition to street names and addresses, pay attention to prominent landmarks and recognizable features when navigating Istanbul. Landmarks like mosques, monuments, and major buildings can serve as helpful reference points for orienting yourself and finding your way around the city.

6. Follow Street Signs: Keep an eye out for street signs, directional arrows, and other navigational cues while exploring Istanbul. Street signs often indicate the names of streets, neighborhoods, and landmarks, helping you confirm your location and stay on course as you navigate the city's streets.

7. Stay Alert and Flexible: While maps provide valuable guidance, it's essential to remain vigilant

and adaptable while navigating Istanbul. Be prepared for unexpected detours, construction zones, and changes in traffic patterns, and be willing to adjust your route or mode of transportation as needed to reach your destination safely and efficiently.

8. Ask for Directions: Don't hesitate to ask locals or fellow travelers for directions or recommendations if you find yourself lost or unsure of where to go. Istanbul's residents are generally friendly and helpful, and many people are willing to offer assistance or point you in the right direction if you need help navigating the city.

9. Keep Your Device Charged: Ensure that your mobile device or navigation device is fully charged before heading out for a day of exploration in Istanbul. Consider bringing a portable charger or power bank to keep your device powered up throughout the day, especially if you plan to rely on maps and navigation apps for extended periods.

10. Stay Safe and Aware: While using maps to navigate Istanbul, prioritize your safety and be mindful of your surroundings. Avoid displaying valuables openly, stick to well-lit and populated areas, and trust your instincts if you feel

uncomfortable or unsure about a particular route or location.

By following these tips and utilizing maps effectively, travelers can navigate Istanbul with confidence and make the most of their time exploring the city's vibrant streets, neighborhoods, and cultural attractions.

CONCLUSION

As we conclude our journey through Istanbul, we reflect on the rich tapestry of experiences, sights, and sounds that make this city truly unique. From its ancient landmarks and bustling markets to its vibrant neighborhoods and mouthwatering cuisine, Istanbul has captured the hearts and imaginations of travelers for centuries, inviting them to explore its history, culture, and beauty.

Throughout this comprehensive travel guide, we've provided you with insider tips, must-see attractions, and off-the-beaten-path adventures to help you make the most of your time in Istanbul. Whether you're a history buff eager to explore ancient ruins or a foodie craving a taste of authentic Turkish cuisine, Istanbul offers something for everyone, inviting you to embark on a journey of discovery and exploration unlike any other.

As you navigate Istanbul's winding streets and bustling bazaars, remember to embrace the spirit of responsible tourism, respecting local customs and traditions, supporting local businesses and communities, and minimizing your impact on the environment. By adopting sustainable practices and cultural sensitivity, you can help preserve Istanbul's unique heritage and ensure that future generations can continue to enjoy its beauty and charm for years to come.

So pack your bags, follow our guide, and embark on an unforgettable adventure through the enchanting streets of Istanbul. Whether you're wandering through the halls of the Hagia Sophia, savoring the flavors of a traditional Turkish breakfast, or cruising along the Bosphorus at sunset, each moment in Istanbul is an opportunity to create memories that will last a lifetime.

Thank you for joining us on this journey, and we hope that this travel guide inspires you to explore, discover, and connect with the magic of Istanbul, where every corner is waiting to be explored, and every experience is a treasure to be cherished. Safe travels, and may your time in Istanbul be filled with wonder, excitement, and unforgettable moments.

<u>Don't forget to kindly rate this travel guide a good 5 star and your reviews. Thanks for reading.</u>

Made in the USA
Las Vegas, NV
22 October 2024

10239907R00075